S & S CYCLE

presents

TODAY'S TOP CUSTOM
BIKE BUILDERS

HOWARD KELLY
PHOTOGRAPHY BY MICHAEL LICHTER
FOREWORD BY JAY LENO

motorbooks

First published in 2009 by Motorbooks, an imprint of
MBI Publishing Company, 400 First Avenue North, Suite 300,
Minneapolis, MN, 55401 USA

MBI Publishing Company titles are also available at discounts
in bulk quantity for industrial or sales-promotional use. For
details write to Special Sales Manager at MBI Publishing
Company, 400 First Avenue North, Suite 300, Minneapolis, MN,
55401 USA

Library of Congress Cataloging-in-Publication Data

Kelly, Howard, 1962-
  S & S Cycle presents today's top custom bike builders /
Howard Kelly ; photographs, Michael Lichter ; foreword, Jay
Leno.
     p. cm.
  ISBN-13: 978-0-7603-3603-8
  ISBN-10: 0-7603-3603-2
  1. Motorcyclists. 2. Mechanics (Persons) 3. Motorcycle
workshops. 4. Home-built motorcycles—Pictorial works. 5.
Motorcycles—Customizing—Pictorial works. I. S & S Cycle. II.
Title. III. Title: Today's top custom bike builders.
  TL440.2.K45 2009
  629.227'50922—dc22
                                     2009017910

On the cover: Odyssey Motorcycle's entrant in the S&S
50th anniversary bash.

On the frontispiece/title page: Check out the intricate
engraving on Covington Cycle City's old-school chopper.

About the author

Howard Kelly, former communications manager for S&S
Cycle, has been editor at *Hot Bike* magazine and at *Street
Chopper* magazine and a staff member at *Hot Rod Harleys*
and *Motorcyclist* magazines. He lives in Onalaska,
Wisconsin.

About the photographer

Michael Lichter's motorcycle photography has been
featured in *Easyriders* magazine for over a quarter of
a century. His photos have also appeared in numerous
Motorbooks titles, including *Indian Larry*, *Choppers:
Heavy Metal Art*, *Top Chops*, *Arlen Ness: Godfather of
Choppers*, *Billy Lane Chop Fiction*, *Harley-Davidson
Century*, and *Sturgis*. He lives in Boulder, Colorado. You
can see more of his work at www.lichterphoto.com.

Editor: Darwin Holmstrom
Designer: Mandy Iverson
Cover Designer: John Barnett/4 Eyes Design

Printed in China

contents

fifty years of proven performance

By Jay Leno

MY FAVORITE TIME IN AMERICAN INDUSTRY was the early 1920s and '30s. Back then guys like Henry Ford and Walter Chrysler would not only engineer cars, they would go out and build them. They touched the product, understood the design, and made sure it worked the way they intended.

When World War II came around, we didn't just win the war because we had the best soldiers; we won because we were also the best industrial nation. We had the technical ability to produce a bomber every hour and the drive to make sure it happened. As a nation, we began building some of the coolest stuff: fast cars, fast motorcycles, and a whole industry of aftermarket performance parts, driven by guys who spoke a similar language—performance. A lot of what I know about S&S makes me respect them, much as I do about the Fords and Chryslers who built this country. When I call S&S I get a guy on the phone who speaks my language, understands what I am trying to do, and because he built my engine, he knows what I'm talking about. S&S is all about American performance. Let me tell you a quick story of how they got that way.

S&S's motto is: "Fifty Years of Proven Performance." Not all 50 of those years were spent touting proven performance, but the tag line has suited S&S for a long time. Back in 1958 S&S got its start when George J. Smith figured out that people would pay him to make their bikes faster. Smith was a sharp guy—he figured out how to make his bike faster than those of everyone else around his Blue Island, Illinois, home. He would spend his weekends dominating at the local drag strip in Half Day Illinois. Smith had another thing going for him besides being a good tuner: his wife Marge ran his business for him. While George tinkered in the shop or worked on the lathe, Marge took care of business, answering calls, writing orders, and doing tech support on the phone. Their business was the stuff American dreams are made of—the chance to make a good living at something they loved. Both George and Marge loved riding, and after they moved the business—and family—to Viola, Wisconsin, in 1969, George built a couple bikes to test parts for himself and then put together a clean '66 Shovel for Marge and him to ride on. Turns out the '66 was a sleeper; it had a set of S&S stroker flywheels and all too often showed its taillight to challengers on the winding roads of Wisconsin, with both George and Marge on it.

When the second generation of S&S family members took over the business, it was a time of change in the motorcycle industry. The custom bike world on the level we now know it was born. Sure customs and choppers had been around forever, but when S&S released the first 96-ci long block, the custom world changed. At the same time the S&S long block hit, a number of frame manufacturers began offering frames with pretty much any rake, stretch, and design a custom builder could want. As the custom builders started showing off what they could do with the 96-incher, demand for Harley-Davidson motorcycles skyrocketed. Obviously owners were going to need to add power—and then customize their bikes to make them stand out.

The surcharge added by the customizing drove the cost of an H-D up some $10,000 or more. This created a business model that transformed S&S from a well-known carburetor manufacturer to the premiere provider of original equipment engines to almost every custom builder. The custom

bike business drove S&S to run two and three shifts from the mid-90s up until about 2004. The demand for their engines was intense, but so were the new EPA regulations on the horizon.

As S&S moved into the third generation of Smith family members, full attention was devoted to building a proprietary engine that would meet future emissions requirements—the X-Wedge. I know a little about this unique engine, as I own a bike with a 117-ci X-Wedge in it. The engineering in it just makes sense. Still air cooled, it uses pushrods but benefits from a 56-degree v-angle, three cams, and a massive one-piece crankshaft. The mass helps reduce vibration, increases low-end torque, and makes my bike a whole lot of fun to ride. Fifty years of proven performance. S&S is far from where they started in 1958—look at the fifty bikes in this book and you can see the past, the present, and the future of what this American icon is going to give the motorcycle industry for the next 50 years.

s&s 50th anniversary celebration

A party for the history books . . .
or history for the party books

FIFTY YEARS AGO, George Smith started a business based on making all motorcycles go faster. That commitment marked the beginning of S&S Cycle. With his wife Marge at his side, Smith founded the motorcycle company that really pioneered the V-twin performance world.

Five decades later, S&S is known around the world for building go-fast parts and go-faster engines. As the company prepared to celebrate its first 50 years in business, a party was in order. But what to do? In fairly short order, a plan was devised to hold the "World's Biggest Build-Off," for which S&S would invite 50 builders from around the world to use 1 of 50 commemorative anniversary engines to build 50 bikes and compete for $50,000.

A group of S&S employees, led by President Brett Smith, sat down with a list of several hundred custom builders and narrowed the list down to 50. It was a long, painful task, but when it was done, the group felt that the list represented a diverse variety of builders from around the globe. Builders were selected from Japan, New Zealand, Australia, Germany, France, Italy, the United Kingdom, Holland, Sweden, Canada, Belgium, and the United States. It was truly a global event.

When the judging by the 50 builders, media representatives, and select VIPs was finished, Keiji Kawakita of Hot-Dock in Tokyo, Japan, was crowned the champion. His bike was a work of engineering art that wowed the builders enough to garner their votes.

The event was held June 27–29, 2008, in La Crosse, Wisconsin, and the facility that hosted the bike show tallied close to 30,000 visitors. Since La Crosse is a community of only 55,000 residents, the riders who came to town increased the town's population by more than 50 percent that weekend. Except for a bit of rain, everything went smoothly, and the city embraced the riders. Additional motorcycle-only parking—closing down 3rd Street to only motorcycle traffic at night—and hotels supplying kickstand pads and towels for bike washing were just a few of the gestures made toward riders coming to La Crosse.

It was an event for the history books. Never before had the motorcycle industry seen a gathering like this: 50 of the world's best builders coming together to share in the spirit of George Smith's dream, celebrate the custom industry, and give people something to talk about for another 50 years.

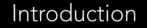 s&s cycle history

BACK IN THE EARLY 1950s, there was no catalog full of hop-up parts for your motorcycle. Making your bike go faster came from cutting parts off and figuring out how to tune the engine better. It was at the latter skill that George Smith Sr. excelled. Smith knew how to tune, and how to make a bike fast. He dedicated his life to making motorcycles go faster.

Smith had a 1939 61-ci Knucklehead, which he initially bumped up to 74 ci and finally to 80 ci by swapping out a stroked crankshaft, longer rods, and bigger cylinders and pistons. Since having more cubic inches requires more gas to run fast, Smith crafted a set of twin-carb heads and bolted on a pair of Riley carbs. The result of this labor would become the *Tramp*, the terror of Half Day drag strip in suburban Chicago. Smith won enough races to gain a following of people who wanted him to work on their bikes.

Smith and Stanley Stankos, a good friend and fellow drag racer, were in demand back in 1958. Everyone seemed to want the pair to make their bikes faster. Soon enough, a company was born, and S&S (Smith and Stankos) started selling its first part—lightweight aluminum pushrods. The new company was filling a need in the market with good old American ingenuity.

After their first year in business, Stankos decided he liked his upholstery business more than the motorcycle industry. Smith's wife Marge encouraged George to buy Stanko's share of the business, which he did, and together the Smiths continued running it. Marge was an

integral partner in the growth and development of S&S, fielding tech calls and handling product sales.

Smith continued racing and developing new performance parts, and in 1966, designed his first carburetor. He knew that the stroker engines he was building needed more fuel, and so to get the necessary carburetor design, he'd have to build it himself. Working closely with Leo Payne, Smith set to work designing and building the perfect racing carburetor. After about a year and a half of hard work, the first S&S carburetors were born. Refinements of that racing carb brought about the first street carbs—an area S&S would specialize in throughout the growth of the business.

In 1968, Smith packed up his family and shop and moved to Viola, Wisconsin. During that first summer in Viola, he, Payne, and Warner Riley went to Bonneville, where Payne ran 203.379 miles per hour, breaking into the prestigious 200 MPH Club. In the

early 1970s at Bonneville, Smith, Riley, Denis Manning, and representatives of Harley-Davidson Inc. set a new land-speed record for a single engine streamliner at an incredible 265.492 miles per hour. Harley-Davidson enlisted factory race star, Cal Rayborn, to pilot the streamliner. An untested streamliner and a neophyte pilot resulted in Rayborn crashing the liner. After watching Rayborn weaving his way through the record run, Smith openly proclaimed him "the bravest man alive."

The early gas carburetor that was designed for racing had gained quite a reputation as a street mixer. George added a choke, refined the lower speed mixture circuits, and designated the model the "L," or late-series carb. The stroker flywheels were redesigned and forged in steel rather than cast iron. A major change for all kits was the addition of TRW forged pistons. TRW had the most advanced technology and had invested more materials into testing its piston alloys than any other company to date. George Smith contracted with TRW to produce pistons for S&S, simply because they were the best available. By 1975, S&S had developed the Super gas carb that became a legend to V-twin racers. Later, a new body casting designated the "B" was added, and the name Super B became generic to the growing number of enthusiastic S&S customers.

In 1975, because of S&S and George Smith's expertise in long-stroke engines, S&S was contacted by the Harley-Davidson motor company and hired to build two 80-ci prototype Shovelhead engines. The motors were

constructed using S&S components and shipped off to Harley-Davidson. The two twins were tested and used in development program that gave riders the 80-ci factory motor, introduced in 1978–1979. Unbeknownst to S&S, Warner Riley was called upon by Harley-Davidson to test the engines at a local drag strip on several occasions. Reports from a Harley factory technician, released years later, said those engines also survived an ungodly number of full-throttle dyno test hours.

When George Smith passed away in 1980, Marge continued running the company with her family supporting her and assuming many roles in growing the business. The Super D race carburetor came to life in 1983 and has been in production ever since. Later in the 1980s, the Evolution engine was introduced, and by 1985, S&S had a full line of stroker kits available for it. "Proven performance" was growing again.

Also, S&S didn't stop going to Bonneville and setting records. In fact, S&S and Manning teamed up again to utilize S&S employee and test rider, Dan Kinsey, to go back to the Great White Dyno, where he cut a new record of 276.510 miles per hour! Kinsey and S&S went back to Bonneville on *Tramp III* and set a partial streamlined record of 238.321 miles per hour. "Performance" and "S&S" were becoming interchangeable words.

In October 1990, the Super E and G carbs were introduced and the market went wild. At one point, there was a waiting list of over 10,000 customers wanting the new performance carbs. Sadly, Marge Smith passed away in 1992, so the second-generation Smith family members took over running the company. In 1994, that team introduced long block engine assemblies that required only a gear cover, rocker boxes, tappets, and tappet guides to be complete. By 1997, the team had developed the rest of the components, and complete S&S engines were available. The market went wild again, which made keeping up with demand a full-time job.

S&S continued to grow, expand, and supply the needs of V-twin performance enthusiasts across the globe throughout the 1990s and up to the 2008 50-year celebration. At no time in its history has S&S ever let go of George Smith's mantra: "I want to make every motorcycle go faster."

Section I

p-series engines

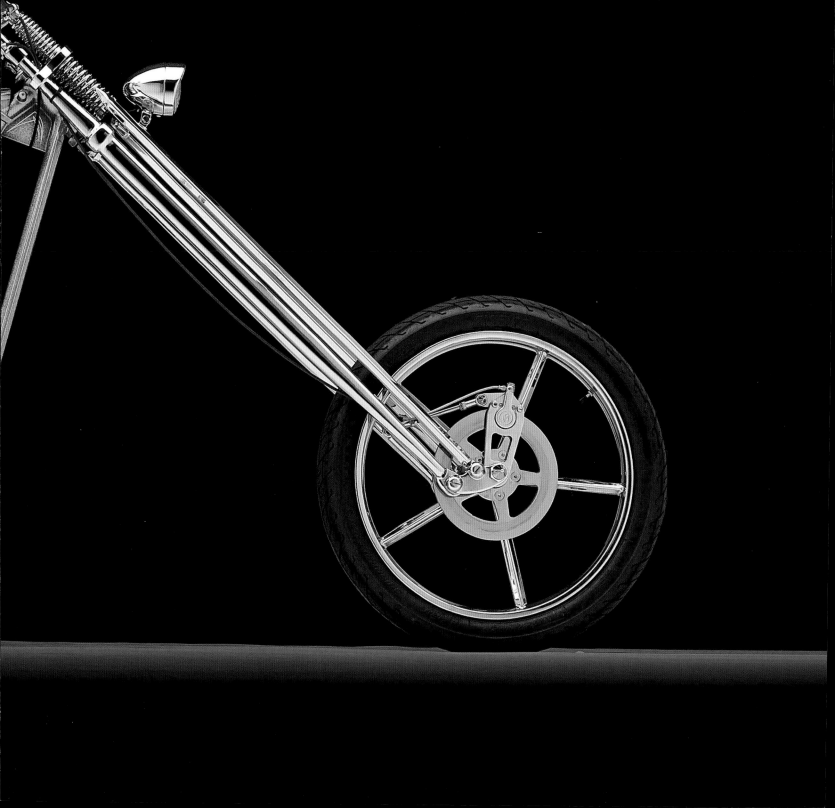

Chapter 1

David Anthony
The Beast

TAKE YOUR TIME WITH THIS BIKE. Dig in deep below the tortured-artist expressionist paint theme on the bike. Go well below the surface and really look at the work that David Anthony put into it. See how his creativity takes the form of a motorcycle that is unlike any other you have ever seen.

Anthony built this bike around an S&S 93-ci P-Series engine fired by an S&S electronic ignition, which is hidden inside the billet timer sticking up from the engine case. Anthony did the air cleaner cover in black to accentuate the black pipes he built for the bike. Black being an underlying theme on the bike, Anthony did the Baker transmission and its end cover in the dark stuff. He tricked out the Belt Drives Ltd. (BDL) primary assembly with a Grandeur auto clutch to make riding the jockey shift bike simple.

To house the potent vintage powerplant, Anthony built a frame with an amazing 50 degrees of rake in the neck. The geometry is made even more radical by the 4 inches of outward stretch and the positioning of a 2-inch-over Jerry's Springer up front. Out back, suspension duties are handled by a pair of SAS shocks connecting to the David Anthony swingarm. Rolling stock consists of a pair of 60-spoke wheels—in black, naturally—with chrome nipples, Avon rubber on the back, and Metzeler on the front. Braking on this unique machine, found in the back, comes from an Exile Cycles Sprotor brake disc–sprocket assembly.

Now, about the sheet metal and paint: David has strong political beliefs that support his artistic thinking. From the collapse of the Twin Towers to a quest for truth, the airbrush work on this bike captures all of Anthony's thoughts. The metalwork, tortured like an artist's beliefs, also tells a story. While it looks like an anvil fell on the bike in places, it also shows just how wild Anthony can be with metal. There is dimension, shape, depth, and creativity in what others may perceive as bent metal. Isn't that exactly what art is supposed to convey?

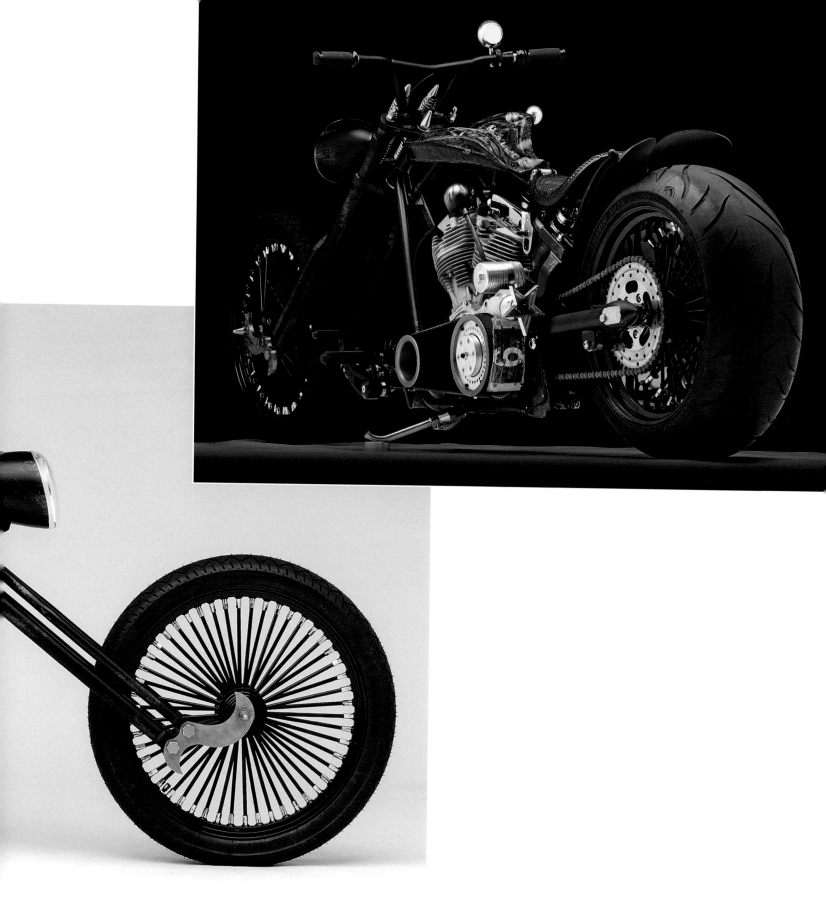

Chapter 2

Branko Built Motorcycles

Panvision

THINGS ARE A LITTLE DIFFERENT DOWN UNDER—Wyong Creek, Australia, to be location-specific—where Branko makes his home and shop. When Branko heard that the S&S 50th Anniversary Celebration rules required the inclusion of some type of S&S tribute, he went full throttle on the idea.

Branko prepped a 1958 Harley frame—the same year S&S was founded—to be the basis of his new design. Adding six degrees of rake to the neck and reconstructing the seat area to be more of a drop-seat design, he also eliminated a bunch of unnecessary tabs and brackets before calling it done. Next he installed the wild-looking spoke wheels he created, featuring gold-plated, diamond-cut spokes wrapped in Metzeler tires.

Turning attention to the driveline, he slid the S&S P-Series into the chassis, added a Baker primary assembly, and managed to make a Baker six-speed "Frankentranny" fit the 50-year-old chassis. Branko built straight dual exhausts for the P-Series and covered the left side with a heat shield resembling the sidewinder snake that is so tied into S&S performance.

Sticking to his early bike theme, Branko refurbished a 1958 H-D gas tank from a scrap heap. Finally, he created a set of saddlebags reminiscent of the period, but functional for a bike like this. After mixing up blue and white paint that resembled Branko's son's drum kit, he sent the bodywork to an airbrush artist named Kriss. Working with photos from the S&S archives, Kriss brought the history of S&S to life on the bike via an airbrush. Branko made handgrips from silver and Navajo Indian turquoise, created a seat from buffalo hide with emu inserts, and added another S&S air cleaner on the primary side of the bike. Even from halfway around the world, Branko's talent as a builder is clear when you look at his bike.

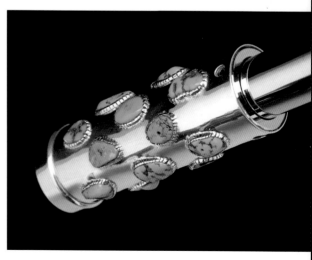

Chapter 3

central coast cycles
Hulk Bike

EVERY ONCE IN A WHILE, OPPORTUNITY POUNDS ON YOUR DOOR. Such is how Scott Long describes the story behind this bike. Within days of each other, S&S and *Chopper Challenge* contacted Long at his Central Coast Cycles shop about doing a bike build—S&S for its 50th anniversary and *Chopper Challenge* for a new television show episode. Long, knowing he couldn't build two bikes for the requests that came practically simultaneously, did the only thing he could do: he convinced both parties that the same bike could fill both roles.

Despite reducing his workload to just one bike, Long realized time still wasn't on his side. The TV show was set to film right up until two days before the S&S event, meaning Long would have to drive from southern California to La Crosse, Wisconsin, in less than two days to be on time. The pressure would be on until he had the bike parked among the other 49 bikes in the S&S 50th Anniversary Celebration.

The good news was that the build went fantastically smoothly. Using a CCC frame as a jump off, Long attached a Kiwi leaf spring fork and a set of Renegade wheels, which he designed for the project. Next he put the high-compression S&S 103-ci P-Series engine in the frame and connected a Baker primary drive and Baker six-speed transmission to it. The only real challenge in this process was building the dual pipes to enhance performance and still look really cool.

Based on what he had done at this point, Long knew that sheetmetal work on the bike had to be less than prominent. The profile of the chassis called for a small gas tank, so he built a deep tunnel version that would hang low on the top tube.

A fabricated oil tank fills the area below the seat and gives the electronics a place to hide. A pair of curved struts supports the short, tire-hugging rear fender. A spring seat gives some ride comfort, and Performance Machine foot controls and a nice, wide set of handlebars offer comfortable ergonomics for such a small bike.

When Long arrived in Wisconsin, he dropped the bike off at the show, hopped in his truck, went straight to his hotel, and slept—the pressure was off and opportunity needed a nap.

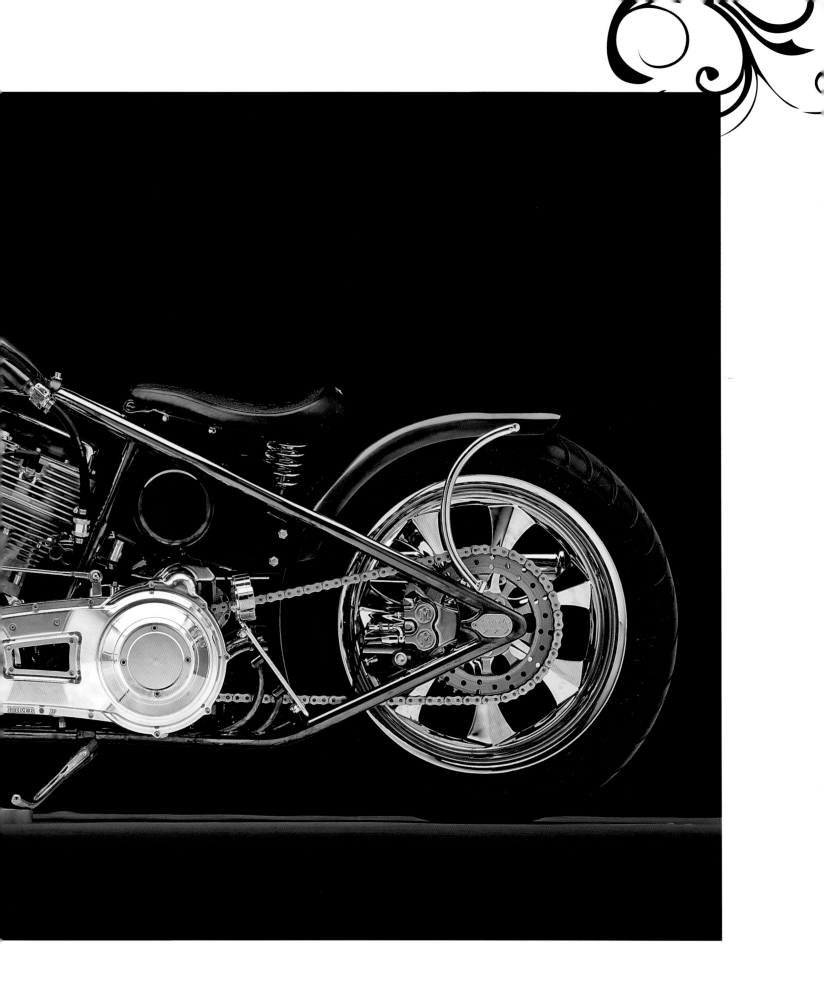

Chapter 4
chica

ORIGINALLY FROM JAPAN AND NOW LOCATED IN HUNTINGTON BEACH, the surf capital of California, Yasuyoshi Chikazawa—better known as "Chica"—combines eastern and western design aesthetics and blends retro styling with modern technology to build bikes that are as intricate and attention grabbing as the best modern sculpture.

Chica went back in time to build this wild chopper around an S&S 93-ci P-Series engine. He started with a Santee rigid frame, and when the sparks cleared, the original 38-degree neck was positioned an extra 6 inches up over its original location, giving the finished product a radical stance. A Paughco 21-inch-over springer fork created a home for the 21-inch Chica wheel and Avon tire, while a matching 16-incher went in the rear. Knowing the P-Series delivers plenty of power, Chica mounted a Performance Machine disc brake up front to compensate for the minimal stopping power provided by the H-D drum in the rear.

Chica went wild dressing up the chassis. He sculpted a prism gas tank, and then segmented a portion of it to incorporate an oil tank. You really don't see it during a quick first glance, but slow down a bit and you'll notice the hard oil lines that connect directly to the oil pump. That design opened up the space under the seat to really show off the prism styling of the rear fender that Chica built directly into the frame. Since he had all that open space under the seat, he decided to keep it, eliminating the battery and using a Joe Hunt magneto to power the electrics instead.

Looking back at the bike, Chica felt it needed another prism styling element, so he built a two-into-one exhaust culminating in a reverse prism shape that looks and works great on the bike. A full-on retro gold paint job done by Buckwild Paint finished off this great-looking bike. The paint design incorporates a small, gold metalflake that surrounds floral stenciling accentuated by tones and shading in the color. Very period correct and attention getting—just as Chica planned.

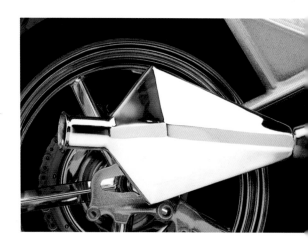

paul cox industries
Sword of Damocles

PAUL COX IS A TALENTED BIKE BUILDER AND LEATHER MANUFACTURER, which is pretty obvious just by looking at some of his work. What most people don't know about Paul is how well read he is, delving off into history and world affairs. He applied a bit of this knowledge when naming his new creation: *Sword of Damocles*. If you don't get it, spend a few minutes on the Internet looking it up.

Cox jumped into this project with a vision in mind—the raw performance of a drag bike tamed just enough to be streetable. First order of business was to customize the engine. Working closely with S&S, he coordinated the assembly of a 93-ci P-Series engine with two front heads. By doing this, it would allow the intake ports to face rearward on both, permitting simple installation of one carburetor per cylinder. It was going to mean a lot more work on a set of custom pipes, but the look, as you can see, is well worth it. Due to his artistic nature, Cox spent an unbelievable amount of time engraving the cam cover on his Panhead, so that at a quick glance you almost think the cover is clear and you are seeing inside the engine.

Next he turned his attention to building a chassis that reflected his vision. Starting with a Paughco rigid frame carrying 30 degrees of rake, Paul added 2.25 inches of upward stretch and plenty of crossbracing. He added a Paul Cox Industries girder front end featuring his "girderdraulic" suspension. A very simple spoked front wheel—devoid of any type of brake—and an H-D wheel out back wrapped in an M&H slick compose the rolling stock.

High atop the frame, Cox fabricated a combination gas and oil tank. Looking at the base of the unit, the fuel supply line and the three oil lines exiting the bottom of the tank are quite interesting. A tiny rear fender with a sporty looking rider brace makes a perfect spot for a Paul Cox seat.

Did you do the research on the sword of Damocles? Great—now the bike's name makes perfect sense, doesn't it?

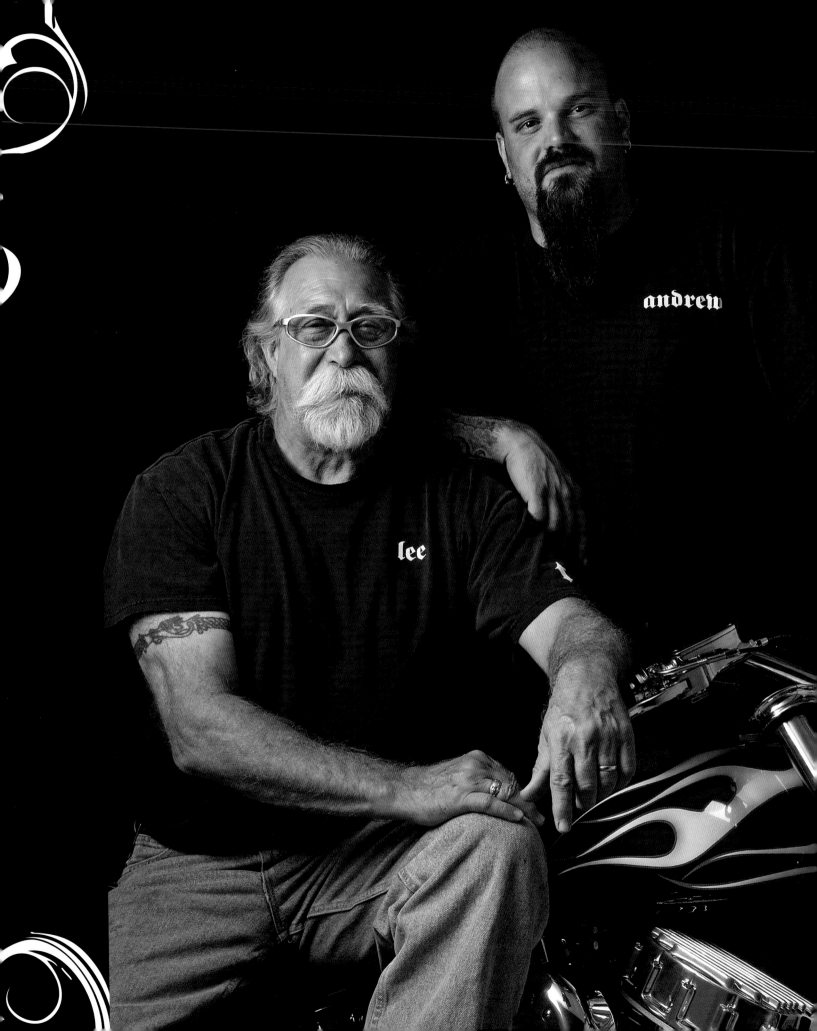

Chapter 6

Departure Bike Works
TLC Forever

LEE CLEMENS AND DEPARTURE BIKE WORKS have been playing the custom-bike-building game for some time now, during which they have seen many things come and go in the custom-bike world. Lots of bodywork, no bodywork, chrome, flat paint, choppers, street racers: Lee has seen it all "cycle" through. One constant he counts on is that people will always love a Panhead. Such is the case with Lee's customer for this bike, Andrew Williams. Not only does he love a Panhead, he also loves Lee's work. Williams signed on to finance the 50th entry, as long as he got to take it home after the event.

The build started with a Motorshop Single Loop frame with 35 degrees of rake and no stretch—the perfect canvas for Clemens. His plan was to fit the engine to the frame so tightly that passersby would wonder how it got in there. A custom front end built by Departure, with a combination of parts from Barney's Speed and Boyd's, set the profile.

Lee positioned the 93-ci P-Series engine in place and took a step back to look things over. It was tight, but not quite what he wanted, so a few tabs were re-welded, an adjustment was made here, another there, and soon enough, the top of the cast rocker cover that he added and the frame were very close. He fabricated a set of pipes to match the curve of the frame, installed a Rivera open belt drive with Departure mid-controls and a Baker six-speed transmission with a hydraulic clutch cover and a kicker, and decided the drivetrain was done.

After installing a set of H-D spoked wheels, Clemens and Williams focused on the styling of the bike. A gorgeous gas tank was shaped to match the lines of the frame, and an ignition switch and flush mounts were built in. Next they worked with Travis Clemens (RIP) to create the unique oil tank whose edges were chased with round bar to add even more dimension. Lastly, they fabbed up the rear fender and featured a drop panel to give Williams battery access.

Once the Page Customs paint and Michael Hall graphics dried, Clemens and Williams started finalizing the build. When they stepped back for a look, it was clear they had nailed it—a custom that would never go out of style.

Chapter 7

HogTech
Swedish Chopper

CHOPPER IS AN OVERUSED WORD IN THE CUSTOM WORLD, but you really could not call the HogTech bike anything but a chopper. The crew from Sweden started this project with a vision for a clean, uncluttered, sleek machine. The plan was to hide every line, wire, and cable possible. Hard parts would be all that would show.

A high-compression S&S 93-ci P-Series engine powers the long and lean chopper. HogTech exhaust pipes and billet rocker covers by Robbans Speed Shop dress up the engine, while inside Super Cycles in the Netherlands did some extra performance blueprinting to extract every last ounce of power. Getting that power to the back wheel is not a chore for the package HogTech put together, which incorporates a BDL 2-inch primary drive assembly and a Baker Franken six-speed kicker tranny. Shifting is done with a jockey shift that has a clutch lever built right into the assembly.

Sheet metal from the HogTech collection dresses up the bike. Considerable modifications were done to HogTech's chopper style tank, which now features a CSC gas cap and nickel-plated decals. The HogTech oil tank is a perfect fit in the frame, but never content to leave anything alone, the crew at HogTech built in an oil temperature gauge. Yet another HogTech part—the rear fender—was utilized to complete the profile of this bike.

With additional bits in place, like HogTech handlebars and foot controls, a Sybo seat, and a Raydon license plate mount, Peter Gustavsson took on the task of hiding all the wiring on the bike. The last step was to have Lindberg apply the Hot-Rod Wine Red Candy and Crème Beige Pearl paint to complete the minimalist chopper. No matter where you look, you won't see any visible part that doesn't seem to be a necessary part of the bike—and that is what a chopper is really all about.

Chapter 8

Krugger Motorcycle company

Half Day

FREDDIE KRUGGER DECIDED FROM THE START HIS BIKE WOULD REFLECT A TRIBUTE TO COMPANY FOUNDER, George Smith. An avid drag racer when he started the company, Smith was the winningest motorcycle rider at a track in Half Day, near his Blue Island, Illinois, home.

With a picture of *Tramp*—Smith's race bike—in mind, Krugger went to work on a frame. Rather than a rigid, he built a Softail with well-hidden pivot points. The tiny chassis was constructed with a single downtube design that doubled as the oil tank. Support for the rear swingarm was done with cleverly mounted Fournales shocks. Beringer calipers provide an amazing amount of braking strength.

Powering his *Half Day* creation is an S&S 93-ci P-Series engine. With an electronic ignition hidden in the timer cup, wild Krugger pipes, and the reliability these engines are known for, it was the perfect choice. Connecting power to the big back wheel is a Pro Clutch belt drive, H-D transmission modified by Krugger, and a chain final drive.

Wrapping around the engine and under the frame is a Krugger-built gas tank that adds a speedy look to the bike. A bobbed rear fender, also Krugger built, barely covers the tall back wheel and hides a taillight in its upward flip. A consistent trim element throughout the bike is the use of drilled panels as heat shields on the pipes and as fillers in the frame neck, seat support, and frame panels. These drilled metal pieces add that look of going fast.

Half Day does a great job of reflecting back to the days when a motorcycle had to do it all: provide transportation on the street, win races, and get the rider back home.

Chapter 9

Cory Ness
Narrow Minded

CORY NESS IS ONE OF THREE NESS FAMILY MEMBERS WHO WERE PART OF THE BUILD. Mentored by the best of the best, his father Arlen, Cory in turn mentored his son Zach. Knowing that not only were his son and father out to win the show, but also were 47 other builders as well, Cory dug in deep for some killer bike ideas he wanted to try.

Trending away from the rest of the world using huge frame tubes, Cory went with 7/8-inch tubing for the core of his project. Then, instead of rigid, he set the frame up to be a rubber-mounted Softail style with 40 degrees of rake and 5 inches of stretch. There definitely would not be another frame like this in the project.

Ensuring individuality, Cory used 23-inch wheels from the Ness facility. These wheels are widest near the axle and taper down; they are unlike any wheel seen before. The gas tank on Cory's bike took quite a bit of pounding and metal shaping to create its dramatic shape. The oil tank mounted to the transmission was fabricated the same way—lots of work, but worth it for the look of this bike. Motivation for Cory's bike comes from an S&S 93-ci P-Series engine equipped with a magneto from Morris Magneto and pipes designed by Cory.

Eric Reyes applied the candy red paint and then did the graphics found all around the custom machine. Cory added pieces from the Ness catalog everywhere that made sense, like the hand and foot controls, oil lines, and even the handlebars that were built into the front end. He topped things off with a Headwinds headlight and a Danny Gray seat before pronouncing his entry done and proving to everyone that he has a style that steps out of the mold.

Trevelen Rabanal
Super Company Customs

No, you are not having a flashback of the late 1960s; you are looking at a bike built in 2008. Look really closely and you will recognize the engine—an S&S 93-ci P-Series equipped with billet rocker covers, magneto by Morris Magneto, and a completely refurbished S&S L carb. If not for the billet-trimmed powerhouse, Trevelen would have you completely believing he hopped in a time machine and brought back a gorgeous rigid.

Working from his shop, SuperCo, located in the heart of East Los Angeles, Trevelen holds onto the roots of cool choppers. He grew up around the East Los Angeles scene, with its stripped-down rigid bobbers, long springer choppers, and always, always a focus on Panheads and Shovelheads. When asked to be part of the S&S 50th Anniversary, Trev jumped at the opportunity to bring his style of retro cool to the show.

Starting with a 1956 H-D rigid frame, Trevelen took the neck out to a respectable 38 degrees before he mounted a 6-inch-over Harley springer on the front of the bike. A pair of spoke wheels, a 21-inch front and a 19-inch rear, give the bike its stance, while a stock H-D drum brake makes a veiled effort at stopping the bike.

Trevelen reworked a Sportster gas tank to sit high on the backbone and leave plenty of space between it and the seat, just like the bikes he grew up with. A standard horseshoe oil tank and hard lines were positioned just ahead of the West-Eagle rear fender. Just in case a passenger wanted to come along, a SuperCo sissy bar rides along in the back.

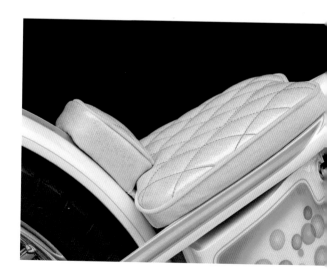

Trevelen handled the wild retro paint scheme in-house at SuperCo, and the closer you get to it, the wilder it looks. A set of Chopper Dave's footpegs, an open belt primary, jockey shift, and a Super C—made seat round out the wild, way-back machine.

Taking in all the detail on Trevelen's bike is a lot easier than building a time machine. Enjoy the ride.

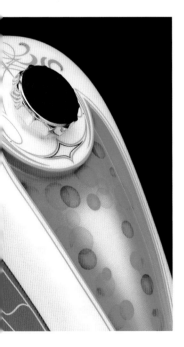

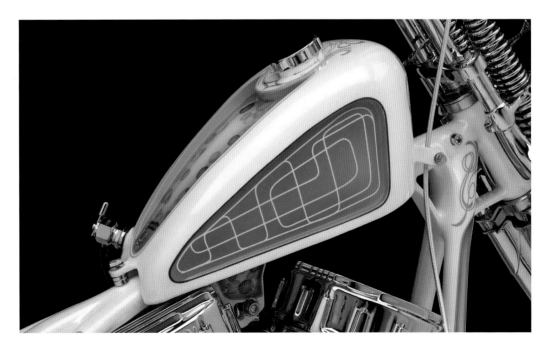

Section II

SB-Series Engines

Chapter 11

Engineering and More
Wakan Track Racer 100

THE ENGINEERING AND MORE (E&M) WAKAN TRACK RACER 100 IS AS FAR FROM A CHOPPER, bobber, or any other kind of custom as a Hyundai is from a Ferrari. Knowing that, it's much better to assess the Track Racer for what it represents: a new model that is ready to be released the minute there is demand for it.

Sleek and compact, the Track Racer is based on an E&M backbone frame with just 22 degrees of rake. The frame utilizes the engine as a stressed member, and when the bodywork is in place, you really can't see the frame at all.

Suspension is a key component on a bike like this, as performance riders expect feedback and control at race speeds. E&M achieves this with a Ceriani 46mm fork up front and a ZF Sachs shock connected to the aluminum swingarm. Marchesini wheels and sticky Michelin radial tires add to the high-speed control of the Track Racer. E&M worked with AJP in Barcelona to come up with a caliper and rotor package that was lightweight and offered incredible braking power.

A good chassis can handle plenty of power, and the Track Racer gets it from an S&S SB100 built to E&M specifications and using an E&M downdraft intake, Devil twin-pipe exhaust, and an ignition built by Dynatech. An E&M primary design with a Gates belt feeds an Andrews five-speed gearset through a Rivera Primo dry clutch, allowing the rider to do wheelies pretty much at will when the throttle is twisted open.

Shame as it is to cover up all the high-tech goodies, E&M has fabricated its own body panels from either roto-molded twin layer composite nylon, or autoclaved carbon fiber. The fairing, tank cover (which actually houses the downdraft intake and air box), and rear seat section (which feeds the twin gas tanks) are all made from these materials. Every element of this bike emphasizes E&M's focus on technology and lightweight construction.

As concept bikes go, the Track Racer leaves very little to desire. A nimble chassis, plenty of power, and incredible looks all packaged in a racer's street-legal dream.

Chapter 12

Krazy Horse Customs
Krazy Racer

READING THE TECH SHEET SUBMITTED BY KRAZY HORSE CUSTOMS' PAUL BEAMISH, it seems every other line says "one-off." If you allow your eyes to take in the details of the *Krazy Racer*, you will see that it is not a stretch in description at all—nothing on this bike is off a shelf, except the S&S 100-ci SB-Series engine.

The Krazy Horse crew worked with Drew Ford to develop the wild-looking cradle frame. The holes are not simply cut out of the frame; there are cylinders inserted and welded inside them to add rigidity, likely making the frame stronger than if the holes were not there. Next, the four-piece swingarm was fabricated with the help of Hariss and Morph of the Krazy Horse team. Satisfied they had a one-off chassis, the team mounted an Ohlins shock at the rear to match up with the Ohlins upside-down fork in Hariss triple trees.

Working with Kustom Tech, Krazy Horse created a pair of 18-inch one-off wheels. The massive hubs aren't covers for the disc brakes, but rather, they house a four-leading shoe brake up front and a twin-leading shoe unit in the back. If all that isn't "one-off" enough, the back wheel is wide enough to accommodate a 240mm Metzeler rear tire!

For the sheetmetal portion of the build, Beamish turned to Parkers for some "aluminium" help, or as we know it in the United States, aluminum. Parkers carefully smoothed the soft metal into a beautiful gas tank and seat pan that complements the frame perfectly.

Rounding out the power package involved building a set of really cool Krazy Horse exhaust pipes, mating the S&S SB100 engine to the Baker six-speed transmission via a 3-inch Nasty belt drive, and installing a final chain drive. To say this bike has the potential to be fast is as obvious as the fact that there are no real off-the-shelf parts on it.

When the bike was unveiled in La Crosse, Wisconsin, at the S&S 50th, there was no mistaking the one-off theme—you won't ever see another bike just like this anywhere!

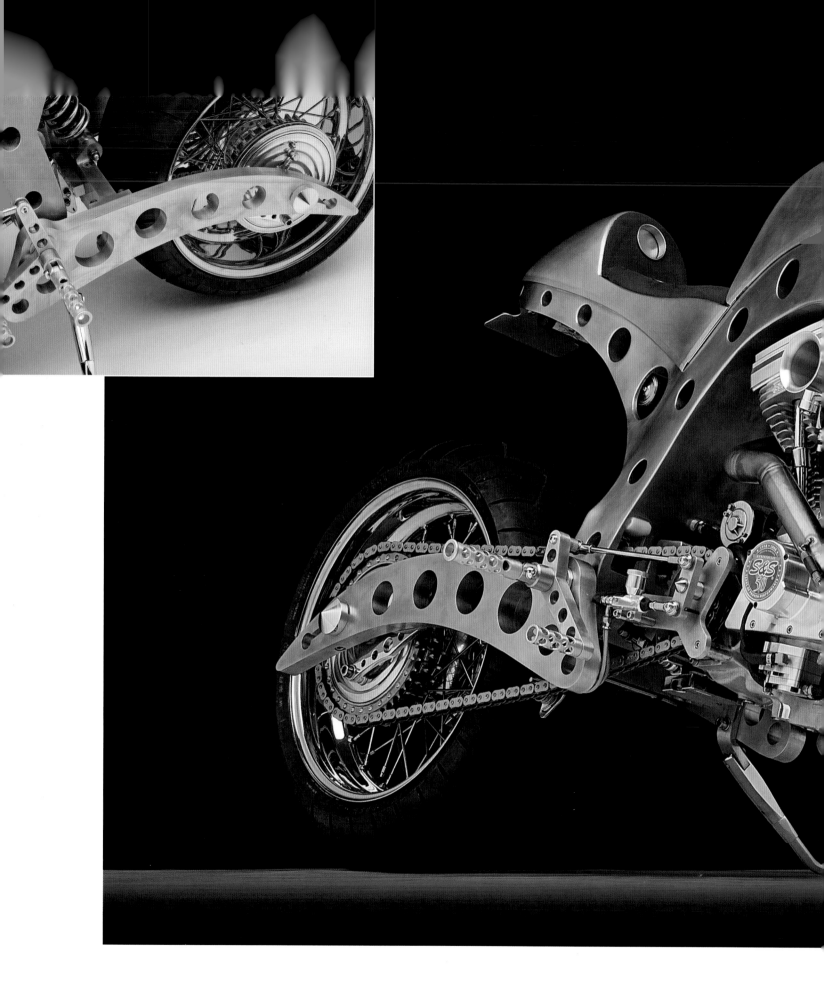

Chapter 13
odyssey motorcycles

IT IS HARD TO BREAK THE RULES WHEN THERE IS ONLY ONE: to include some type of S&S tribute. Bertrand Dubet and his Odyssey Motorcycles shop basically started from a clean sheet of paper when asked to participate in the S&S 50th Anniversary. They had an SB engine and a desire to win the show—a pretty potent combination for this shop, based in Toulouse, France.

The project started with the construction of a frame that would incorporate the S&S SB100 as a stressed member. This permits the overall profile height of the bike to be lower, since there is no need to allow for clearance for a bottom support tube. Connected to the huge tube frame is an Odyssey-built swingarm that utilizes a set of Fournales shocks to soften the road's irregularities. Up front, a very unique-looking Fournales girder fork assembly leads the bike.

To dress up this engine/chassis package, the guys at Odyssey went to the parts room and brought a Crime Scene Choppers gas tank to the workshop. A little trimming, cutting, and shaping later, and it was the perfect complement to the chassis. The rear fender was hand-formed from some flat steel stock in the shop. What? No oil tank? It is there; it's just built into the massive tube frame, adding to the sweet, sleek look.

A very special set of 21-inch OMP wheels was built for this bike and gives it a sporting look. These wheels house perimeter rotors, front and rear. The rotors were cut with the S&S logo all the way around, in keeping with the theme of the show. If you look closely, you can see the OMP calipers front and rear, but they are almost hidden in the design of the bike.

Rounding out the fine details on this amazing creation are a headlight from a Chevy, hand and foot controls from OMP, Odyssey-made pipes, and a winning attitude. And it did win the SB class at the 50th anniversary show, because attitude and desire are everything!

Chapter 14
Prugh Design
Silas

THE STORY BEHIND MICHAEL PRUGH'S BIKE *SILAS* IS MUCH MORE INVOLVED THAN THE CONSTRUCTION OF THE BIKE. On the weekend of the S&S 50th Anniversary, Prugh called me 24 hours before he was due at the show announcing his bike was not finished. A few parts he was awaiting back from some outside vendors had not shown up, so his bike was incomplete and he didn't think he should show up. I encouraged him to show anyway, knowing what his bike was going to be.

Prugh did show up and brought most of *Silas* with him. Built around an S&S 100-ci SB-Series engine, he utilized a modified H-D transmission, clutch, and primary assembly to complete the package. Prugh created an exhaust system that complements the bike without overwhelming the rawness of the powerplant.

Naturally, Prugh built his own chassis, which uses three main parts. The 27-degree neck rides in front of a twin-spar design and carries the oil supply in its tubes. You don't see many XL-style bikes with a Softail rear-suspension design, but Prugh made it look natural, with the swingarm extending out of the bottom frame tubes and creating the illusion of a continuous piece. To roll the project around, Prugh fabricated his own wheels, 21- and 20-inch, equipped with perimeter brakes at both ends.

When dressing the chassis up, he used a minimalist approach for *Silas*. A basic XL tank from Custom Chrome, Inc. (CCI) and modified by Cole Foster and Prugh, and a pair of fenders that started life as Jim Nasi blanks, were all that were needed. Prugh built the battery mount into the swingarm as a structural component.

To complete the bike, Prugh built handlebars to sit atop the Buell front fork and V-Rod headlamp. Out back, a Todd's taillight provided visibility, while a Kreun Kustom seat provided the balance to the Nissin hand controls and Prugh mid-controls.

Prugh exhibited guts and pride in his design by showing up at the event with a half-complete bike. The final product shows why he had reason to be confident.

Chapter 15
Redneck Engineering
S&S 50th Tribute Bike

THE BUILDER OF THE BIKE ON THESE PAGES IS REDNECK ENGINEERING (RE), whose name alone should conjure up a vision of a machine far from being as polished as this is. Funny name aside, the team at RE is very serious about its designs and keeping things cost-effective for customers. It builds a number of bike kits that allow the use of original engines, suspensions, and wheels to save a few dollars.

The *S&S 50th Tribute Bike*, though, was not crafted to save a single dollar, but rather to push the design team further. Starting with the frame, the team used decreasing dimension elliptical tubing and integrated the engine as a stressed member. Neck angle is set at a radical 44 degrees, with 3 inches of stretch in the backbone that doubles as an oil tank. Suspension in the front is an RE tubular springer—2 inches over—and out back is a Progressive Suspension shock that works in a mono-shock application.

To complete the high-tech machine, the RE team sculpted a flowing gas tank that stretches from the steering neck all the way down past the seat post. A rear fender that barely covers the huge 23-inch wheel was fabbed, and then a set of RE DropChop mini-ape hangers was added. The whole package was shipped out to Carolina Customs for the paintwork.

Road worthiness came about when the last bolts on the Performance Machine hand and foot controls, drag headlamp, Outlaw Customs leather-covered seat, and the Nasty bike clutch and primary assemblies were installed. Hopefully by this time you have figured out the name of the company is either misleading or Redneck Engineering stands for something toward which more of us should aspire.

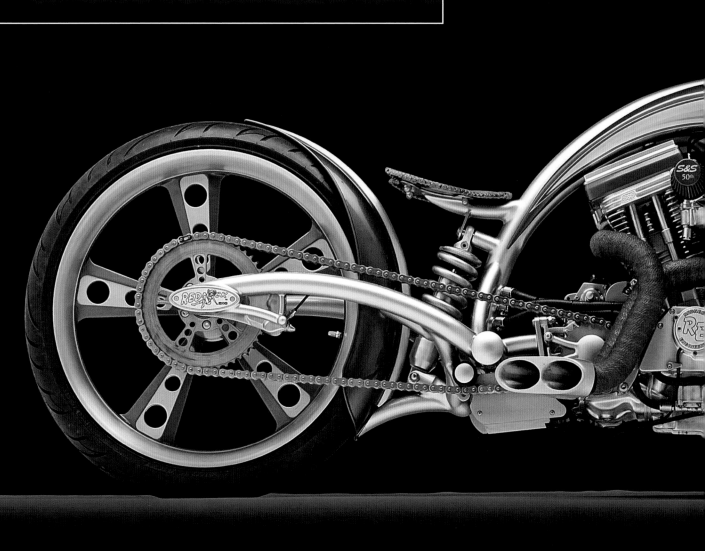

Chapter 16

Jesse Rooke

ONE LOOK AT JESSE ROOKE'S 50TH ANNIVERSARY BIKE AND YOU MIGHT THINK IT ISN'T FINISHED. Well a funny thing about that—it is and it isn't. About two weeks prior to the event, a call came through to my office from a television crew that wanted to make sure it was OK to film Jesse wrapping up his bike at S&S just before the bike show. Of course the answer was "yes." A week later, a small box arrived at my office to the attention of Jesse Rooke. Five days before the kick-off of the show, Jesse showed up in my office and asked about the parts he shipped. I handed him the small box. "What about the frame, engine, wheels, and all the other stuff that was shipped?" Rooke asked. I had no answer. He dug in on the phone and found out it would all arrive in another day. The bike was in parts, not assembled, meaning Jesse would have just three days to get it together.

With a TV crew over his shoulder and many S&S employees and other builders pitching in, Rooke went to work putting the Paughco Sportster frame on a bench, adding a Marzocchi 40mm fork and a set of 21-inch KTM wheels on it. Next, he installed the S&S SB100 engine with the Baker six-speed gearset and the Tech Cycle belt drive. It was starting to come together, even if it had no paint anywhere.

From deep within the parts box, he pulled out a Storz aluminum XR-style gas tank, an L-Tec oil tank, and a rear fender that Dennis Sanchez had shaped for him. Then Rooke added some dirt-track-styled exhaust pipes, which he had worked on with Todd Silicato and which looked perfect on the project. Next, a set of all-terrain vehicle (ATV) handlebars, some universal dirt bike hand controls, and a seat pan on springs was added. Working late into the night Thursday and early morning Friday, Rooke finished the bike and added the S&S 50th Anniversary emblems on the tank.

So when you look at Jesse's bike, it is either finished or not finished to you, but for a three-day marathon, it's not bad at all.

Chapter 17

stonebridge motor company
Little Miss Dynamite

A LONG TIME AGO, there was a group of motorcycle riders who raced around England on bikes called café racers. These bikes, light and powerful, were measured by their ability to hit the "ton" (go 100 miles per hour) and handle leaning deep into turns like a race bike. These riders ended up hanging around a place named the Ace Cafe. Just down the road from the Ace, now managed by Mark Wilsmore, is a stone bridge, which has become a reference point for people getting directions to the café. In between the two landmarks is Nick Gale's Custom Cycles.

Gale had a dream of bringing back the café racer with a proper version sporting a big engine, great frame, and minimum of everything else. Using an S&S SB100—an engine capable of delivering more than enough horsepower to get a bike well past the ton—Gale went to work on a frame to accommodate the engine. Drawing inspiration from the famed Norton Featherbed frame, Gale fabricated the Super Wideline Featherbed frame for the project. He mated an Ohlins fork assembly to the 29 degree neck, and connected a pair of Ohlins shocks to the tubular swingarm. As could be expected, bodywork on *Little Miss Dynamite* is minimal. Gale worked with the Tank Shop to create the shimmering aluminum tank, held down in the traditional way with a metal strap.

Cool finishing touches, like a sporty open primary assembly, massive tach in the rider's face, and a reverse mount S&S air intake, assure onlookers of the real intention of this bike: to take the rider back to a time when things were simple and breaking 100 miles per hour was all it took to make the world's problems go away.

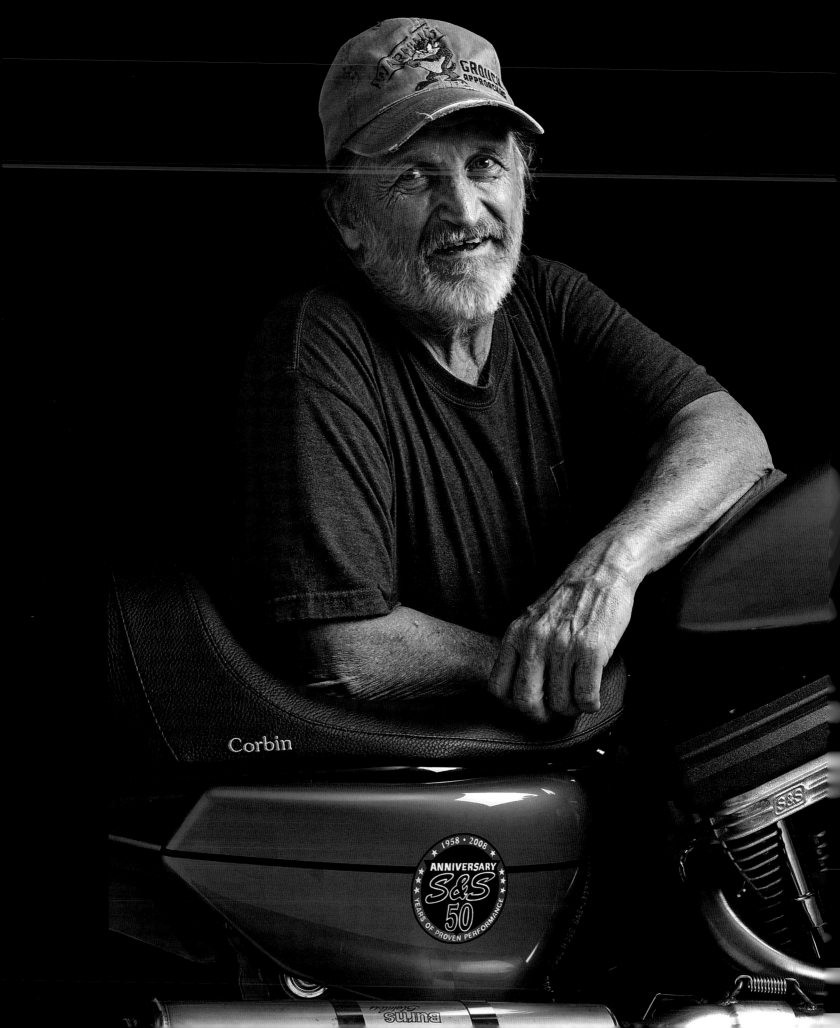

skeeter todd
Pro Street Sportster

NOT ONE TO DO WHAT EVERYONE ELSE IS DOING, Skeeter Todd has made quite a name for himself building custom bikes that incorporate his two favorite features—power and subtlety. Rather than do anything on a bike that draws attention, Skeeter looks for a better way to hide his custom tricks behind the guise of stock appearance. Look no further than this page for a prime example of his "style."

The average custom bike fan will automatically dismiss this as a Sportster and never notice all the Skeeterisms throughout its design. Starting with the frame, Skeeter took a 1979 H-D frame and gave it a 2008 upgrade. Larger tubing, rubber engine mounts, a drop seat, and plenty of reinforcement were the first areas of focus. Forks from a Buell Cyclone were adapted to the frame, and a swingarm and suspension from a Honda sportbike were modified to work in the rear. Boyd's wheels, Avon tires, and Jaybrake calipers combined to create the rolling stock.

Reinforcing the frame made sense, as that old 1979 XL put out about 50 or so horsepower, while the S&S SB100 that Skeeter was building around is capable of double that, plus a few extra ponies. Skeeter got extra horsepower from the combination SuperTrapp/Burns exhaust he built for his bike. A seemingly stock H-D primary case was modified to accommodate the Honda swingarm, and a 2001 H-D gearset was used to fill the transmission cavity.

Fuel is held in a cleaned-up 3.6-gallon Sportster gas tank, and oil is carried in an oil tank custom-made to fit in the unusual frame design. Keeping rocks and mud off Skeeter's face is a fender that was rescued from a junk pile. In the back, a 1999 Indian fender was trimmed down to match the lines of the bike. The last metalwork Skeeter did was to fabricate the side panels that filled in the gap in the new/old frame.

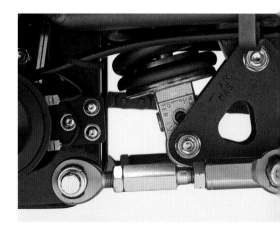

With a subtle but beautiful paint scheme created by Dave Davies, Skeeter seems to have hit another grand slam with this bike: great looks and handling, minimal amounts of that which doesn't make the bike go or stop, and details worth investigating everywhere you look.

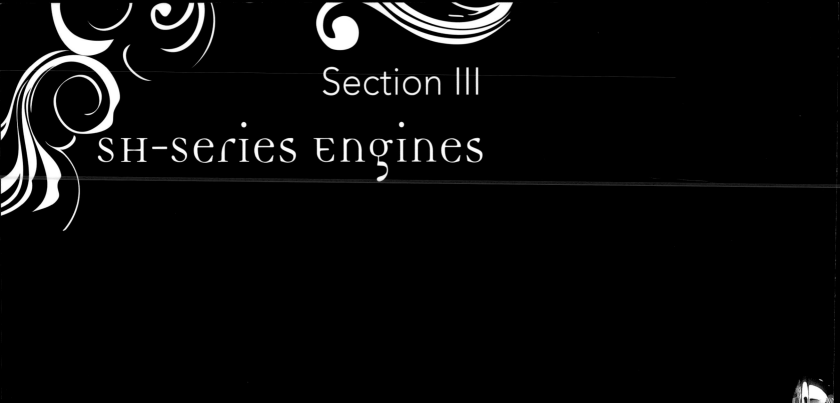

SH-series Engines

Chapter 19
church of choppers

WHEN YOU NAME YOUR SHOP CHURCH OF CHOPPERS, well, choppers better be your deal. For Jeff Wright, choppers—in the true sense of the word—are exactly his thing. A bike that has nothing it doesn't need on it, no extra anything, is what he is all about. His tribute to the S&S 50th Anniversary is a real representation of the bikes he likes to build.

Jeff's small shop employs . . . Jeff. So he does it all and does it his way, even when filling out a tech sheet. Rather than give away any of the specifics on his bike, he chose a lot of one-word answers that mostly agree that various components are on his bike.

Looking the bike over, it is obvious that the Paughco frame he mentions was modified quite a bit. It doesn't seem to have a lot of rake, probably no more than 32 or 33 degrees, but Wright had to add at least 8 inches to the downtubes and some additional fabrication on the top engine mount and the neck. With the stretch in the frame came a need for the 35mm fork tubes to be extended appropriately. Hickman Racing triple trees hold the legs in place, and a set of wheels—very cool looking, but listed just as "wheels" on the tech sheet—with Dunlop tires and plenty of brakes were installed.

Wright dropped the S&S 93-ci SH-Series engine in place and decided that a Joe Hunt magneto was the way to go. He paired the engine with a Baker six-in-a-four transmission by using a Tech Cycle open-chain primary.

The sheet metal on Wright's bike was built in-house. The gas tank is small, the oil tank shiny, and the rear fender and tail section nonexistent; the minimal amount of words on a tech sheet seem to match the minimalism of this bike. About the time Wright had everything in place, it became very apparent that his ergonomic design had a problem. The high-mounted mid-controls he wanted to use wouldn't allow for a rear brake pedal. Wright delved into the roadracing world and installed a rear brake thumb lever, just below the left handgrip, on the incredibly small handlebar he used on his bike.

While there is not much technical information specifically about Wright's creation, it's easy to see how it fits in the category "chopper."

cook customs

THE PARTS USED TO CREATE THE COOK CUSTOMS ENTRY IN THE S&S 50TH ANNIVERSARY CELEBRATION SHOW REAL DIVERSITY. Bits and pieces came from a number of major players in the motorcycle industry, but almost everything was touched in one way or another by the Cook Customs team.

Dave Cook started the build off with a vision of a wild board-track racer—with plenty of twists. Starting in the frame area, Cook and his team built their version of a board-track racer with a Softail-style swingarm, 35 degrees of rake, and a raised backbone to mount the gas tank under it. Next they created a Cook Customs Banana Girder front end and mounted a set of 23-inch, 40-spoke wheels with Cook perimeter rotors.

To dress up the one-of-a-kind chassis, the Cook crew worked with Westbury Handcrafted Motorcycles to come up with the beautiful nickel-plated gas tank that rode under the top frame tube. With the oil tank hidden under the transmission area and no front fender, all it took was a D&D/Fat Katz rear fender to complete the bodywork.

Since easy is just too easy, Dave decided to mate the S&S 93-ci SH-Series engine to a Norton transmission. Not only that, the shifting of the transmission was being switched from the right side to the left—a clear challenge complicated by the need to figure out a primary that would work. With a little engineering and a few trips to Farm and Fleet, the Cook crew made a BDL system work.

Once the engineering was figured out, the remainder of the project followed the standard Cook Customs bike process: add quality components customized for this bike, then stand back and watch it draw a crowd. When Dave and the crew unveiled this machine at the 50th event, it drew a crowd from morning until night.

Chapter 21
Covingtons Cycle City

For the S&S 50th, Jerry Covington and his crew went old school—but with a cutting edge. Covingtons Cycle City does not build just one style of bike—its goes from radical choppers to custom retro cool. To create this bike, it pulled influences from all of the directions it had ever gone and brought it together in one sweet-looking package.

To start the build, the crew tore down an S&S 93-ci SH-Series engine and engraved it in all the right places. The intricate etching shows extraordinary attention to detail: for example, the S&S motto "Proven Performance" is engraved on the cam cover. Covington mated the 93-inch engine to a Baker six-speed transmission with a kick starter—naturally a Covington-modified piece—and a belt drive primary.

The driveline rides in a 1958–1964-style FL frame. A minimal suspension situates this ride low to the ground. Up front, a Covington-customized Perse Performance fork takes care of suspension duties, while out back, Progressive Suspension shocks, likewise treated to some Covington customization, carry the day. The resulting stance sits the bike just right for the 21-inch front and 17-inch rear Covington Hotshots wheels wrapped up in Avon rubber.

Once the crew mounted modified Klock Werks fenders and built a gas tank and headlight nacelle from scratch, it handed everything over to Dusty Brown and Brian Loker to add the Candy Cobalt Blue and Pearl White gloss paint. When the fumes settled down, the resulting paint scheme was the perfect backdrop for an S&S logo.

Details abound on this machine. Seemingly every trim piece, along with the wheels, rotors, and fender struts, carries the same drilled and milled pattern. The combination of classic bike styling, blended with modern billet components, helps this bike transcend time and styling boundaries.

Chapter 22

Bill Dodge
Model 71

It took just three months for Bill Dodge, the man behind Bling's Cycle, to bring *Model 71* to life. In that time, he pretty much built everything on the bike to fit the vision in his head. That is the advantage of being the guy in charge at your shop; you can build it like you want it and not have to listen to anyone—and doing what he wants is the motivation that keeps Dodge's bikes fresh.

The design of *Model 71* links back to a set of Husqvarna dirt bike forks Dodge had lying around the shop. He felt their look would make a perfect match for a board-track-styled bike—with a little extra bling to make it his. Starting with the frame as priority number one, Dodge bent, shaped, and welded tubing until he had a piece with a 32-degree rake and 2 extra inches of rear stretch setting the profile of his bike. Next, 23-inch wheels with Bridgestone off-road tires were positioned at both ends to add to the board-track look.

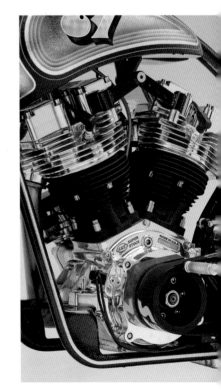

Dodge started making the minimalist bodywork next. He pounded out a gas tank, small enough to blend into the lines of the bike and curved enough to add dimension, and mounted it under the top frame rail. Having a front fender just wouldn't have looked right, and the rear needed to be small, similar to what you might find on a hillclimb bike, while still having enough strength to do the job of carrying a taillight. With body and frame down, he turned to the powerplant.

With such a lightweight machine, any engine would make it feel fast, but Dodge doesn't mess around. He selected an S&S 103-ci SH-Series with high compression and dual plugged heads. The 103 kicks its power through a Tech Cycle open primary and into a Baker torque box. While working in the drivetrain area, Dodge adapted a Baker oil pan to his chassis.

Bling's Cycle is the shop's name, so the Robert Pradki paintwork had to represent the shop. And it does, with bright red and big, thick metalflake chunks. *Model 71* is a vision that came to life just the way Bill Dodge wanted it.

keiji kawakita
StG Nautilus

In Japan, you don't just customize—you build the parts you will use to customize in order for your bike to really be custom. At Hot-Dock, Keiji Kawakita's shop, the only purchased parts for a custom are those Kawakita cannot make himself. And that doesn't mean that any store-bought parts are exempt from modification, as evidenced by his creation for the S&S 50th Anniversary. It was the grand champion, by the way.

Starting with an S&S SH-Series engine, Kawakita went to work customizing it with his own design of fuel injection, special rocker boxes, and a few other cosmetic trick parts. He installed the 93-incher into a frame he built specifically for the design of this bike, with 27 degrees of rake and 2 inches removed from the downtubes to enhance the small look of the bike. To make the frame even more interesting, Kawakita used aluminum tubing for its construction.

The rest of the bike was built in-house at Hot-Dock. Take a good look at the gas cap; it has more detail than most standard bikes have in their whole package. Look at the rear fender and taillight combination. Everywhere your eyes land, you will recognize the intense labor that went into the construction. Even the hardware used to assemble the parts looks custom. Actually, anywhere you look you will see the detail that impressed all 50 builders enough to crown him champion at the big S&S event, and that is as impressive an accomplishment in the motorcycle world as we have seen in a long time.

Chapter 24
zach ness

WHEN YOUR FATHER IS ONE OF THE WORLD'S MOST WELL-KNOWN CUSTOM BIKE BUILDERS, learning the trade is pretty easy. When your grandfather is also the world's most famous custom bike builder, the pressure to build a really cool bike and establish your own style goes up dramatically. Zach Ness could explain it to you; his father Cory Ness and his grandfather Arlen Ness taught him a lot, but he still has had to carve out his own style to get noticed.

Zach was scheduled to start building his bike much earlier than the 25 days he actually used to build it, but he broke his back about the time he should have started. Once he was basically healed, Zach grabbed an old Arlen Ness frame from the 1970s and started cutting and welding. When he finished, the retro chassis was carrying 40 degrees of rake, 5 inches of stretch, and smooth curves in the downtubes. After installing a simple Ness 41mm telescopic fork in Ness trees, Zach mounted a pair of 23-inch Ness billet wheels with Avon tires. The front stops with a Ness caliper and rotor, while the rear features a 360-degree brake in the hub.

To motivate his new creation, Zach installed an S&S 93-ci SH-Series engine with a magneto to simplify the electronics. A Ness open belt primary connects to a Ness transmission equipped with a kick start. Sticking with his simplified theme, Zach's bike is a kick only, so getting the magneto dialed in was really important. He got the help needed from his dad and grandfather.

Back to making his own style stand out, Zach started bending some metal to create a flowing gas tank that tapered into the backbone of the frame. He added a deep curve in the front section of the tank that tied into the shapes he incorporated in the fenders, creating continuity and extra style points. Zach then worked with Eric Reyes to design the stoic paint scheme that set off the brilliant chrome trim on his bike.

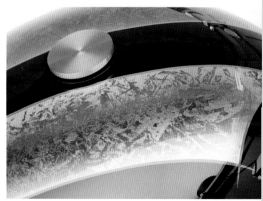

Looking at the bike Zach built in just 25 days, there is no doubt he was taught well growing up. Whether he developed his own impressive style is not even a question that needs to be asked.

Chapter 25
chris olson
Remember

THERE WAS A TIME, not that long ago really, when long, thin choppers dominated the motorcycle landscape. Those days of peace, love, and groovy bellbottoms on choppers were the impetus for many of us to drop an extra 12, 16, or even 24 inches of tubing on the end of our Schwinn Stingrays and pretend we were piloting Shovelhead choppers down the highway.

Chris Olson wanted to build a bike that was as period-correct to that time as possible, so he started by sourcing out a team of people who were there when the coolest period in chopperdom ever took place. The frame for his bike came from Ron Paugh at Paughco, an authority on those chopper-crazed days, and was set to extend the neck 6 inches up, 3 inches out, and lay way back at 45 degrees. To that, Olson added another way-back-when part, a Harmon girder—a whopping 30 inches over—built by Bill Holland. Where Olson scored the Invader Wheels is a mystery, but they fit the bill perfectly.

Powering his machine is an S&S 93-ci SH-Series engine, with period-correct pipes from Paughco. A covered Primo chain drive primary connects to an authentic H-D four-speed transmission. Covering up the chassis was a simple process: add a gas tank, oil tank, and rear fender. The whole package came straight out of the Paughco catalog, unchanged from when it was first offered almost 30 years ago.

Olson built a sissy bar, handlebars, and railroad spike pegs in his Chris Olson Custom shop, sent everything out for chrome, and dropped off the frame and metalwork with Dick DeBenedictis for the wild chunk metalflake paint. DeBenedictis did an amazing job of bringing back the history of choppers in a single paint job. The swirls, color changes, and pinstriping make you really wonder if this is a new bike or a restored barn find—it just looks perfect for the period.

Olson aptly named his re-creation *Remember*, and during the S&S 50th Anniversary, he had a group of riders from back in time surrounding his machine, complimenting the authenticity of his work. He couldn't have asked for more.

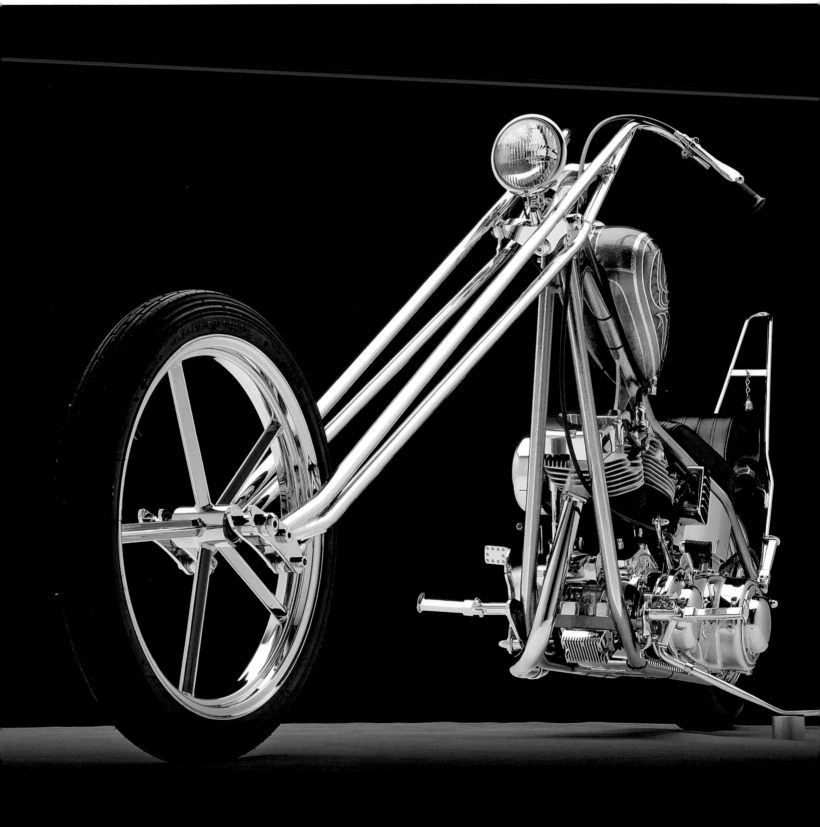

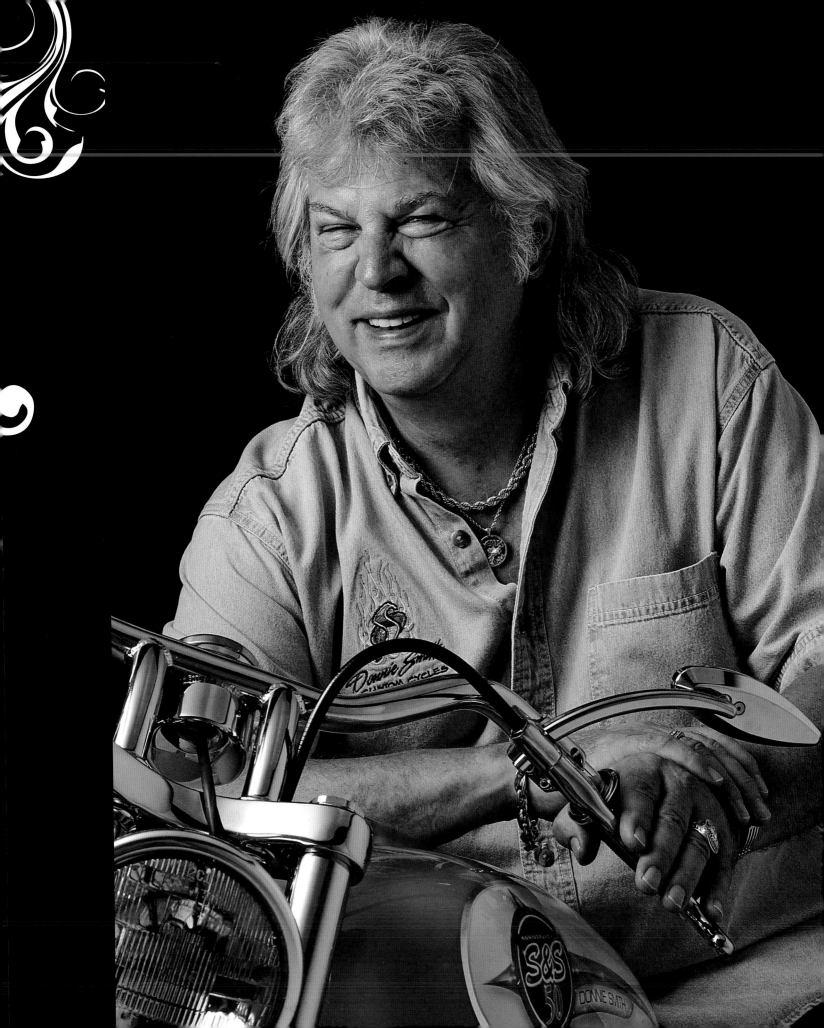

Chapter 26

Donnie Smith custom cycles

DONNIE SMITH ENTERED THE S&S 50TH ANNIVERSARY CELEBRATION with the intention of building a 2008 version of the bikes he built when getting started in the custom bike world. The goal was simple: build a clean custom, much like things were back in the days when Smith began a build with a stock bike, stripped it down, and finished it properly.

With this vision in mind, Smith met with Rob Roehl, his longtime fabrication specialist, and put a plan in motion. They started by ordering a Cycle Craft frame with 36 degrees of rake and 1 1/4 inches of stretch to it. Sticking with their modify-a-stock-bike theme, the pair treated a set of H-D fork legs and triple trees to some *NC Machine* tweaks for cleanup and better looks. Out back, Smith pulled a set of Smith Brothers and Fetrow (SBF) strut shocks out of the closet and matched them up to a swingarm built at his shop.

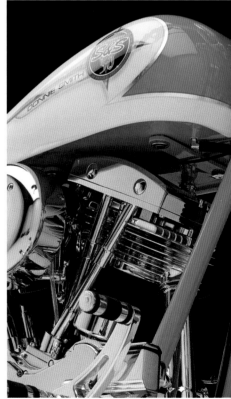

Looking backwards in time, and in the old parts room of the shop, Smith found a set of Performance Machine Cal mags. The front was an 18-inch, the rear a 15, but Smith sent the rear wheel to Sandy Kosman to be redone as a 16-incher. Metzeler tires and a combination of GMA Engineering and Exile Cycles brakes gave the chassis mobility and stopping power.

The S&S 103-ci SH-Series engine was a natural for Smith. It provided plenty of nostalgia to complement the bike's style, but had so much more power than what was available back in the time when bikes like this roamed the streets. Horsepower moved to the back wheel through a BDL belt drive and H-D five-speed transmission.

To create a canvas for the Krazy Kolors paintwork, Smith and Roehl built a gorgeous gas tank that incorporated a Hot Match gas cap and a CCI oil tank (shortened by 3/4 inch). They then modified an H-D front fender and reworked a D&D rear fender. The result of these efforts is a gorgeous bike built in 2008 that looks like it would fit in perfectly in 1980.

Chapter 27
special parts supply
Speed Demon

HOLLAND MAY NOT BE THE COUNTRY YOU AUTOMATICALLY THINK OF WHEN YOUR THOUGHTS TURN TO PERFORMANCE MOTORCYCLES, but the crew at Special Parts Supply (SPS) has plans to change that. This creation, *Speed Demon*, is the shop's best effort at making the lightest, coolest, raciest Shovelhead you have ever seen.

The project started with a pile of tubing that needed to be bent into a frame with as few straight lines as possible. Working slowly and meticulously, the SPS crew came up with a curved chassis that has 34 degrees of rake and a 3-inch drop in the neck, carries the engine oil in the tubes, and looks like the rear utilizes suspension, even though it is a rigid. An SPS Shorty custom was built to look like part of the frame, and a set of 21-inch wheels were created in-house to complete the chassis.

Power is drawn from an S&S 93-ci SH-Series engine with an S&S Super Stock ignition and serious performance pipes made at SPS. A very open chain drive primary connects to a Baker Torquebox six-speed transmission with an SPS/H-D clutch assembly. Of note in the powertrain package design is how the transmission is tilted up to shorten its length, complementing the tiny proportions of the *Speed Demon*.

The steel gas tank flows down over the top frame tube, to almost rest directly on top of the rocker boxes. One side of the tank features engine-turned stainless steel, while the other side is adorned with aluminum louvers. The rear fender is aluminum and polished to a brilliant finish. Turning to Hugo Design Studio, the SPS crew requested the paint be Shelby Blue and Ivory White and for it to flow around the tank badges it built.

With the addition of a headlamp mounted down below the steering neck on the fork, an SPS taillight, and board-track-style SPS bars, the bike was done. Look at *Speed Demon* from every angle possible; no matter where you look, the bike says performance. Holland may be on its way toward being known for something else besides brothels and legal weed.

Chapter 28
sucker punch sallys

WHEN DONNIE LOOS AND THE SUCKER PUNCH SALLYS TEAM WANTED TO CREATE THEIR 50TH ANNIVERSARY TRIBUTE BIKE, inspiration came from all the years S&S went to the drag strip to test parts. Back then, a drag bike was long and lean, emphasizing the focus of going from point A to point B as fast as possible—and that still is the case today.

Donnie built the bike in his head first, and then put a Sucker Punch rigid frame with 38 degrees of rake and 3 inches of stretch up on the workbench. The crew performed a couple of tweaks to the frame, like raising the rear axle to lower the profile and fabricating a new top engine mount.

Taking performance seriously, Loos worked with the S&S crew to have a 103-ci SH-Series engine built with knife-edge flywheels. When it was in the shop at Sucker Punch, the heads were ported for additional performance and a set of Donnie Loos–built pipes were added.

Dressing up the sleek chassis is, well, not much, for it would defeat the purpose of the bike. A simple CCI Sportster-style tank was equipped with a Greg Westbury hot-rod gas cap and a Kustomwerks rear fender. Supporting the fender and emphasizing the theme is a set of Sucker Punch Hot Rod Fender Struts. The oil tank is from Led Sled Customs and is finished in nickel to match many of the other components on the bike. Armstrong Design laid down the blue paint and applied the aptly worded graphics so Loos could move onto final assembly.

Performance was the game, so forward controls made no sense. Instead, Loos mounted mid-controls that allowed him to ride aggressively, along with low-profile drag bars, and finished off the build with an Expertise Auto Interiors–made seat. Having seen the bike run around La Crosse, Wisconsin, during the anniversary celebration, I am convinced it does the job it was intended to do, very well!

Section IV

v-series engines

Chapter 29

Nicolas Chauvin
Wild Night

IT STARTS WITH A WORKSHOP FULL OF RAW METAL: tubing, sheet metal, chunks of aluminum, everything you would imagine that building a motorcycle would require. Then an artist walks into the room, picks up one of the pieces from the pile, and starts shaping it—slowly bending, adding shape, definition, and life to the cold steel. Hours later, the artist straightens up and looks at what he has accomplished—a start to an incredible motorcycle. Such is the story with every bike Nicolas Chauvin has built. The routine is always the same, but the results are spectacular and different with each build.

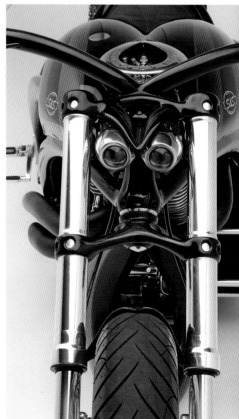

Since Chauvin speaks fluent French and minimal English, getting the story behind his bike is a challenge. But if you let your eyes take in the motorcycle, you can probably picture it yourself. Chauvin had to start building the frame first, coming up with the skeleton to support the body. Look close enough and you can see hints of traditional frame work in it, but his skill at metalworking conceals most of the frame by blending it into the body.

Curves and points seem to dominate the bike, but none are so aggressive that they draw your eye to one spot. Rather, the lines go in different directions, while still allowing your eyes to focus naturally on the whole bike rather than a specific part.

Essentially, the only parts not built by Chauvin are the S&S V124, Baker right-side drive transmission, Ultima belt drive, Barnett clutch, Lightcon wheels, and Avon tires. The rest of the bike was pretty much built by Chauvin, or so heavily modified by him that you couldn't identify a given piece as a stock part.

Unique features, like an electronic fuel pump, an air intake that snorkels up through the top of the frame, LED lighting in the rear of the frame, and a host of other hidden intricacies, give the artist more credit. "Artist" seems to be the right word for the builder of this bike. Wouldn't you agree?

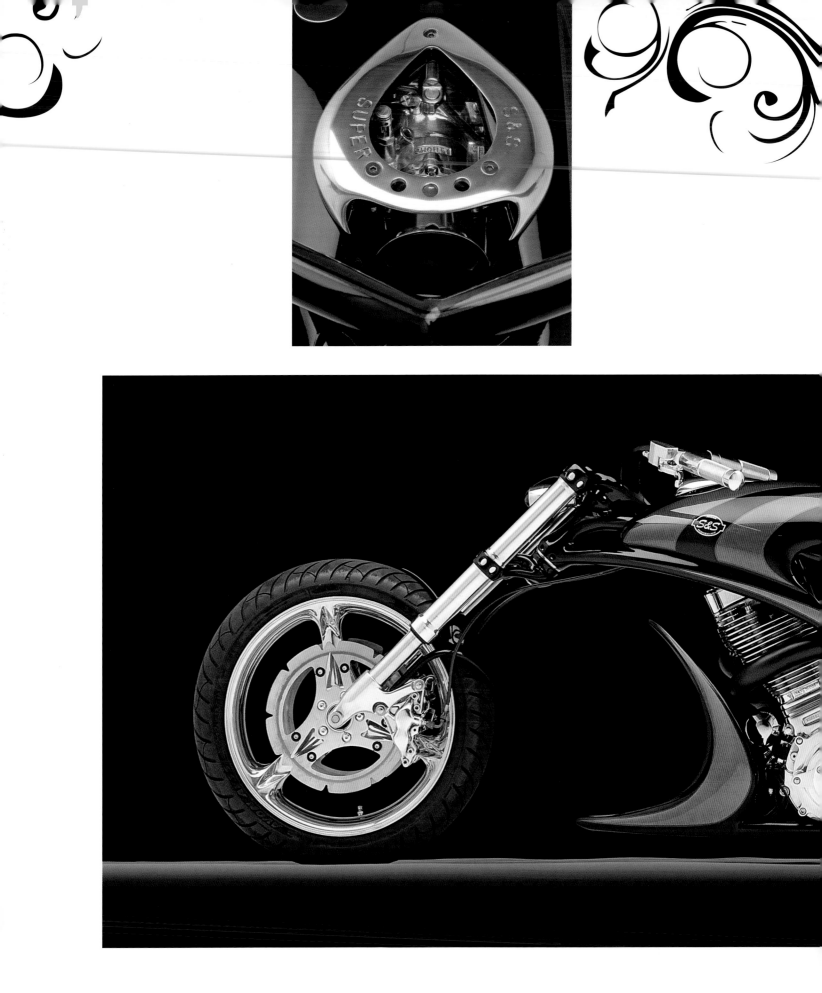

Chapter 30
flyrite choppers
Reach for the Sky

WHEN INVITED TO BE PART OF THE S&S 50TH ANNIVERSARY CELEBRATION, Jason Kidd of Flyrite Choppers had a great marketing idea. He knew the event would get publicity all over the world and that some of the wildest bikes in the world would be part of the show. Betting that there would be very few production motorcycles in the show, he decided to use a Flyrite Choppers Reach for the Sky model for his entry.

The move paid off for Kidd. There are literally hundreds of pages of magazine coverage on the event, and everyone knows you can buy a bike identical to this one for under $18,000. The paint jobs of some of the bikes in the event alone cost close to that much.

The Reach for the Sky model is built around an 96-ci S&S V-Series engine, Primo open belt drive, and a RevTech transmission equipped with a kick start. Flyrite Choppers pipes extend all the way back on the bike, creating a very old-school look.

A simple rigid frame with a 30-degree neck and no stretch forms the core of the bike. It was created with a set of 41mm fork legs that had been dropped 2 inches, and then the lower legs had been shaved of all the extra tabs. Rolling stock consists of a set of black spoke 21- and 16-inch wheels wrapped up in a fat whitewall rear tire and a skinny black sidewall front for a vintage hot rod look.

It is no surprise that the bike pulls its name from the handlebars, which ride way above the thin Flyrite seat covered by Debra Lawson at Redneck Leather. Even with the spring mounting, the seat is a long way from the bars. With a Flyrite 5-inch flat fender supported by a NeveRust fender strut, Sportster-style gas tank, and some minimal pinstriping done by Dan Barnett under the clear powder coat, this bike is an affordable part of history.

Chapter 31

Kendall Johnson Customs

PICTURE YOURSELF AT A TRAFFIC LIGHT PULLING UP NEXT TO THIS BIKE. You look over, see a bagger, and think, "I can easily smoke a bagger. I think I'll go for it!" Don't feel bad, though, as the "bagger" you thought would be so easy to beat screams away from you on its back wheel; this is just another example of what Zach and Kendall Johnson do.

Kendall started his shop a long time ago, and as his son Zach grew up in the shop, he learned about performance and going fast. Soon enough, Zach was drag racing the bikes Kendall built, and before anyone realized it, Zach was a big part of Kendall's business.

Putting together bikes that look good, but maybe don't look as fast as they really are, is a Kendall Johnson Customs (KJC) specialty. In the old days, hot rodders called them "sleepers," and the bagger on these pages is a prime example.

Certainly a good-looking bike, this machine has all the right good-looking parts: a set of Redneck Engineering bags, KJC-built gas tank and fenders, and a Sportzilla fairing by Hoppe Industries. This collection is attached to a Chopper Guys rubber mount frame and supported by Precision Metal Fab Racing (PMFR) wheels and Metzeler tires—the rear being 240mm wide for a reason.

The reason for the 240mm rear? An S&S 126-ci engine, tweaked to all levels of tweaking by KJC. Kendall and Zach know some tricks about tuning an engine to exactly what their customers are looking for, and in the case of this bagger, the bike had to be able to do huge wheelies and smoke people off the line. They backed up the power with a chain primary, Barnett Performance clutch, and a Baker right-side drive transmission.

Street racers, beware of the sleeper, especially if you see a bike bearing the KJC killer clown logo in the paintwork; if you try to race it, you will probably lose.

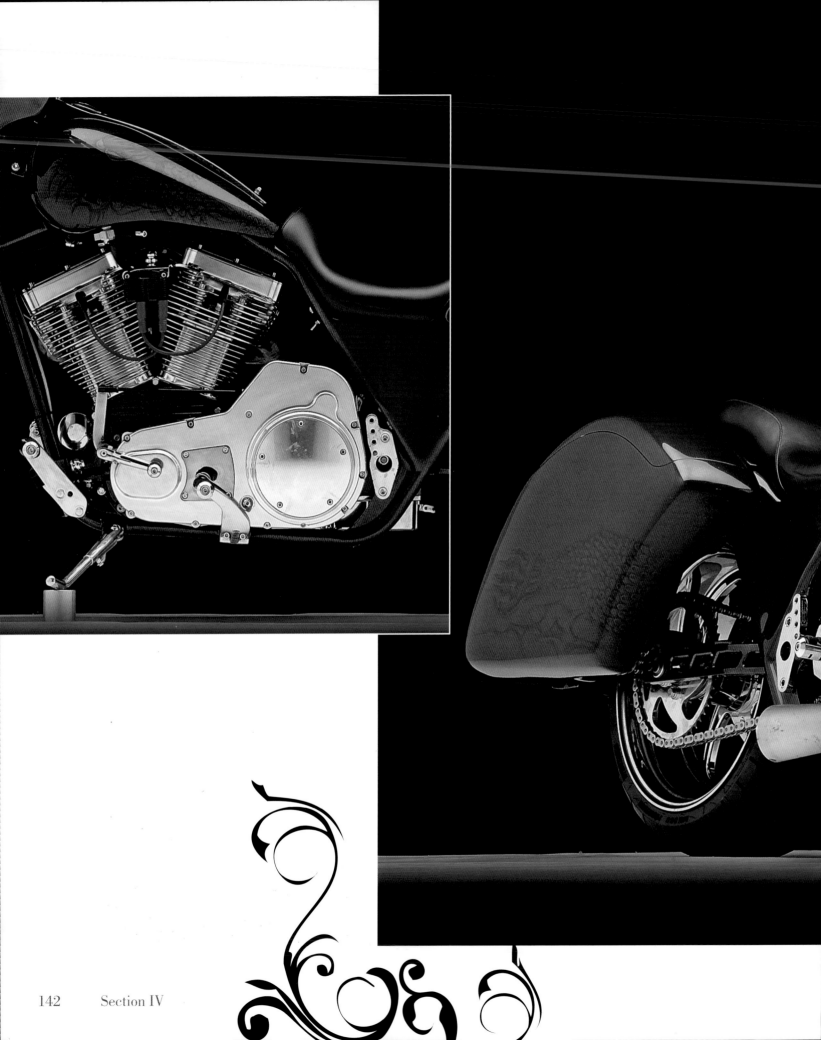

Chapter 32

Kris Krome
D.E.S. 1

YOUR FIRST GLANCE AT THE *D.E.S. 1* THAT KRIS KROME CREATED SHOULD LEAVE YOU WANTING MORE: more pictures, more information, more ways to figure out how you could ride it. Intriguing styling, spartan design, and a clear sense of performance dominate the persona of the bike.

Krome used a 145-ci V-Series, the biggest production engine S&S makes. This engine routinely gets tuned to produce upwards of 180 horsepower at the rear wheel, leaving no question what the results of a drag race will be. Krome ensured that he would have that kind of performance by working with Kendall Johnson on his tune-up. Once he had the engine in his shop, Krome built the frame and swingarm to the specs he had in mind for this project, including carrying oil in the tubes. Up front, he installed a front end that uses suspension Krome refers to as "elastomer," and he used this same process on the swingarm as well.

Satisfied that he had the right tone for performance in his chassis, Krome built an unusual fuel tank that rises up out of the frame and blends forward into a fairing panel below the steering neck. With the known power of the 145, a seat that holds the rider in place was a must, so Krome put it together with a styling hint from sportbikes of the late 1970s, which perfectly complemented his 2008 machine.

Psycho Customs applied the Oh So Sexy Red paint and the gold lettering accentuating the color, and the seat cover was constructed by Mad Cow Custom Leather. Once it was installed, Krome went out for a ride. Even as a brand-new, not broken-in engine, the power was obvious. The shame was that as soon as he confirmed it rode properly, Krome had to rush to La Crosse to make it for the event—but his first ride left him wanting more.

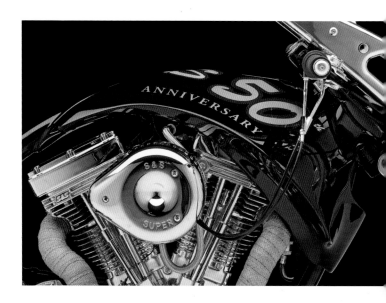

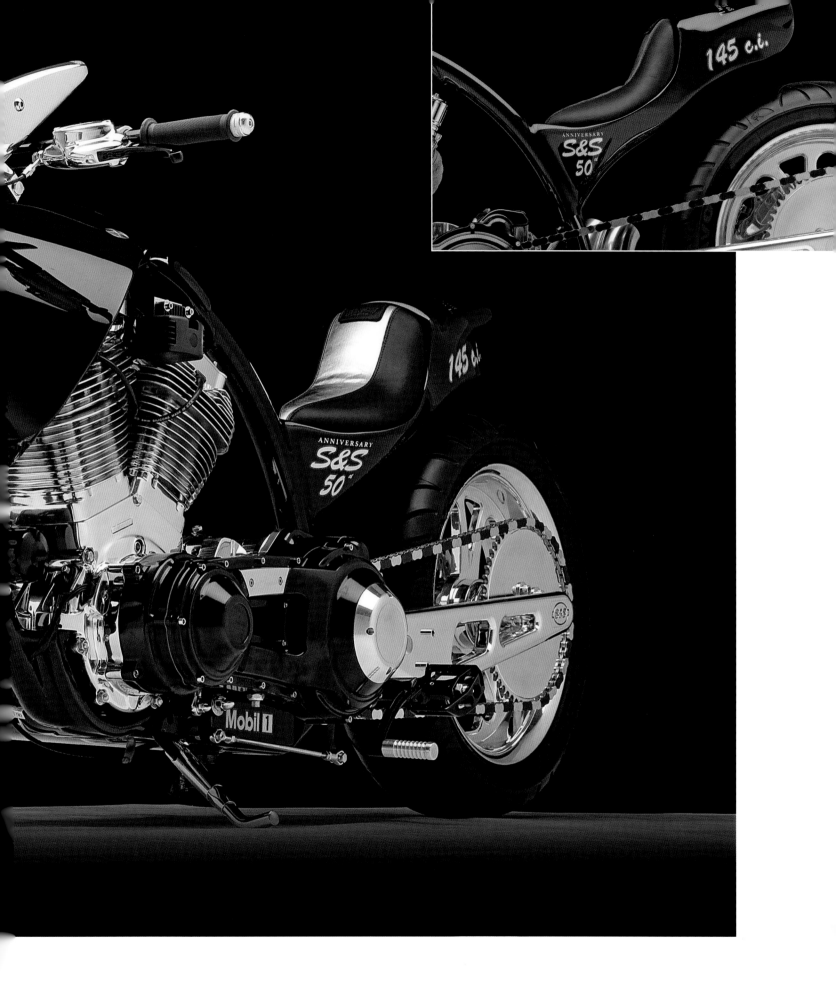

Chapter 33
Arlen Ness

A<small>RLEN</small> N<small>ESS</small>, <small>BY FAR THE MOST WELL-KNOWN BUILDER IN THE</small> S&S 50<small>TH</small> A<small>NNIVERSARY</small> C<small>ELEBRATION</small>, is a man many young builders look up to, but two in particular really hold him in a special place: his son Cory and grandson Zach, both of whom were in the contest. So not only would Arlen need to build a bike cool enough to beat 47 other builders, he also had to keep it semi-secret from his own family. Talk about a challenge!

Most projects are built around the frame of a bike because the frame creates the lines, stance, and profile. Then the bike gets buried with accessories and the frame is forgotten. Ness decided that the frame of his new bike would not only set the tone, but it would also become the focus of the build. Not hiding the tubes under bodywork gives the frame freedom to dominate.

First Ness created a basically conventional rigid frame with 6 inches of stretch and 40 degrees of rake in the steering neck. The backbone curved from the neck all the way down to the lower frame rail section in one graceful arc. Ness then worked with his team to create a combination lower frame rail/arcing fuel tank for each side of the frame. With the fuel tucked down low in the split tanks, the engine would stand out tall, proud, and powerful.

In the case of Ness' new project, the engine doesn't just look powerful, it is powerful. An S&S V124 equipped with a custom Dell'Orto carb setup that the Ness crew created brings in plenty of air and fuel. A Primo open belt drive connects to an H-D Dyna transmission that also holds the oil tank. To slow the big engine down, Arlen built brakes from 360 Brakes into the 21- and 23-inch wheel hubs.

All of the orange on the bike is not painted, but rather powder-coated by Daytec. The orange powder coating makes a wonderful canvas for Steve Farone's graphic paintwork. Accessories that are not fabricated by the Ness crew are straight out of the Ness catalog, including the 2-inch-under springer. When the bikes were unveiled during the S&S 50th Anniversary, Arlen lived up to his reputation. The only mystery was if he managed to keep the bike a secret from his family.

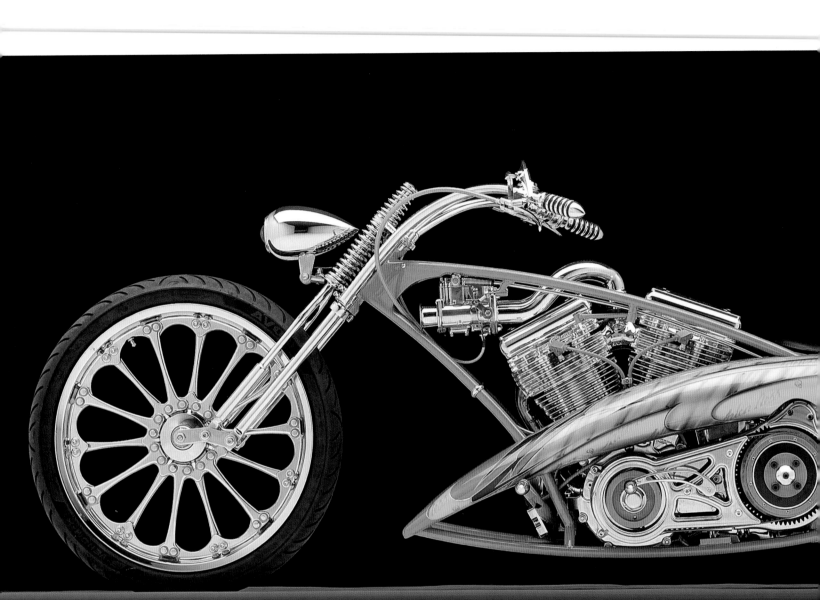

Chapter 34

Revolution Manufacturing
CFXSS-1

REVOLUTION MANUFACTURING MADE ITS NAME WHEN IT BROKE INTO THE CUSTOM MOTORCYCLE INDUSTRY with something not seen before: carbon fiber frames and wheels. From the day Mike Kamalian decided Revolution was able to manufacture those parts, the company has been busy.

For his entry into the S&S 50th Anniversary, Kamalian went straight to his most well-known part—a carbon fiber frame—for a platform. His rigid bike bore a neck angle of 32 degrees, with an additional 2 inches of stretch in the backbone, but 2 inches cut out of the downtubes for a lower profile.

By working with carbon fiber instead of steel, he was able to build a frame that featured curves and shapes not possible otherwise. The rear section of the frame has a gorgeous flow that makes it look like the rear axle sits high, even though it doesn't. Up front, a flared panel creates the look of a splash pan under the engine, but it really just adds strength to the chassis.

Kamalian built the wheels from carbon fiber and wrapped them in Metzeler tires. He connected the front wheel to the frame with a 54mm fork assembly from Revolution Manufacturing, and then went to work on creating radial mount calipers for the bike. To really test the strength of his frame, Kamalian used an S&S V124 engine.

A gas tank that Revolution built, which uses an internal aluminum fuel cell that is surrounded by billet tank covers bearing an S&S 50th Anniversary logo, dresses up the already exotic chassis and blends into the carbon fiber backbone of the frame. A combination seat–rear fender was formed from carbon fiber to finish out the flowing bodylines.

Certainly not common, and definitely not typical, the CFXSS-1 is clearly a revolution in bike building.

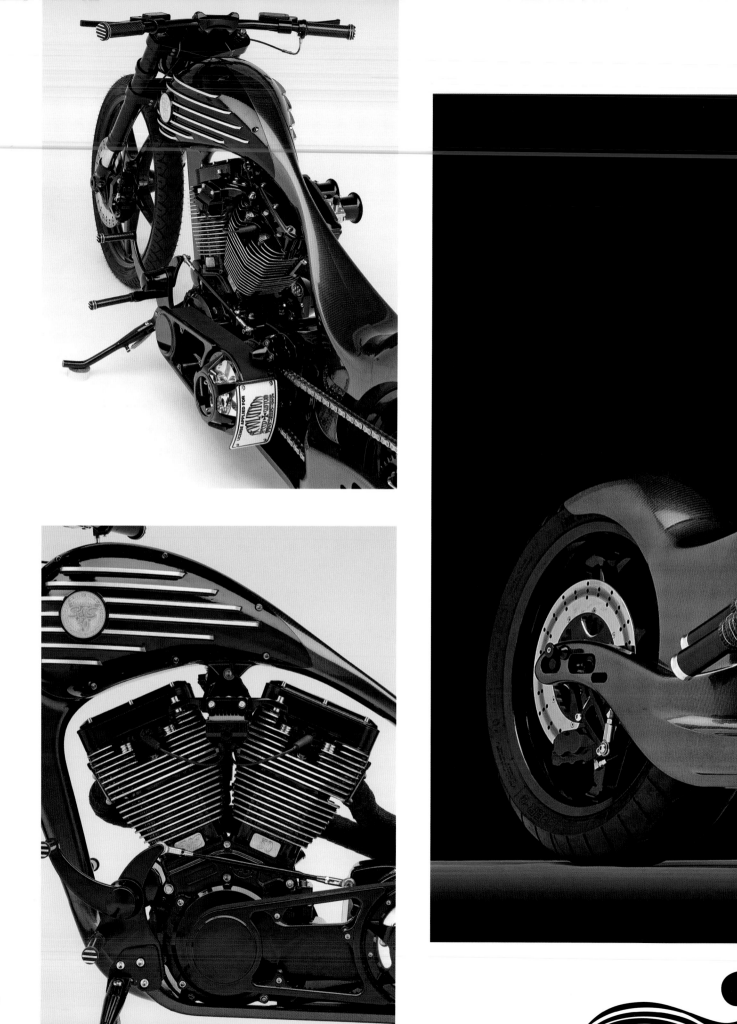

Chapter 35
sabers specialties

GET A LOOK AT THIS SLAMMED-TO-THE-GROUND BIKE BUILT BY SABERS SPECIALTIES, and from any angle, you can't help but focus on the gigantic 300-series rear tire. Massive and meaty, it dominates the bike, clearly emphasizing its ability to get power to the road.

When Blake Sabers—the "Sabers" in "Sabers Specialties"—joined in the S&S 50th Anniversary Celebration, he wanted a big-bore and big-stroke combination that would bring him plenty of power. He got it by using an S&S V124, an engine typically good for about 130-plus horsepower! Backing up that much power is a Primo/Independent Cycle primary assembly and a Baker billet-chrome six-speed transmission with a chain final drive.

There was no fooling around when the Sabers Specialties crew picked out the frame for its anniversary machine. The crew used an Independent Cycle Hardlife drop neck. The frame has 36 degrees of rake in the neck with 5 inches of backbone stretch coming together with a 2-inch-under downtube. To support the front of the bike, a Perse fork assembly is captured in HHI trees and holds a Ride Rite spoke wheel.

Adding some skin to the frame was done with an Independent Cycle gas tank and a pair of Twisted Choppers fenders. The Sabers Specialties team put its own signature on both, by adding some extra shape and dimension to blend everything into the frame. Looking for an oil tank? Look closely under the transmission and you will find the Independent Cycle design tank as part of the frame.

Once the Customs Plus royal blue paint dried, it was time to finish building the bike. Flanders drag bars in Joker risers are equipped with Performance Machine hand controls up top. Below, a set of Independent Cycle controls make a place to hang your feet. The Sabers crew did its job on accentuating the rear of this bike. The only problem with the big 300 rear tire is that you can't see it when you are hauling butt down the road.

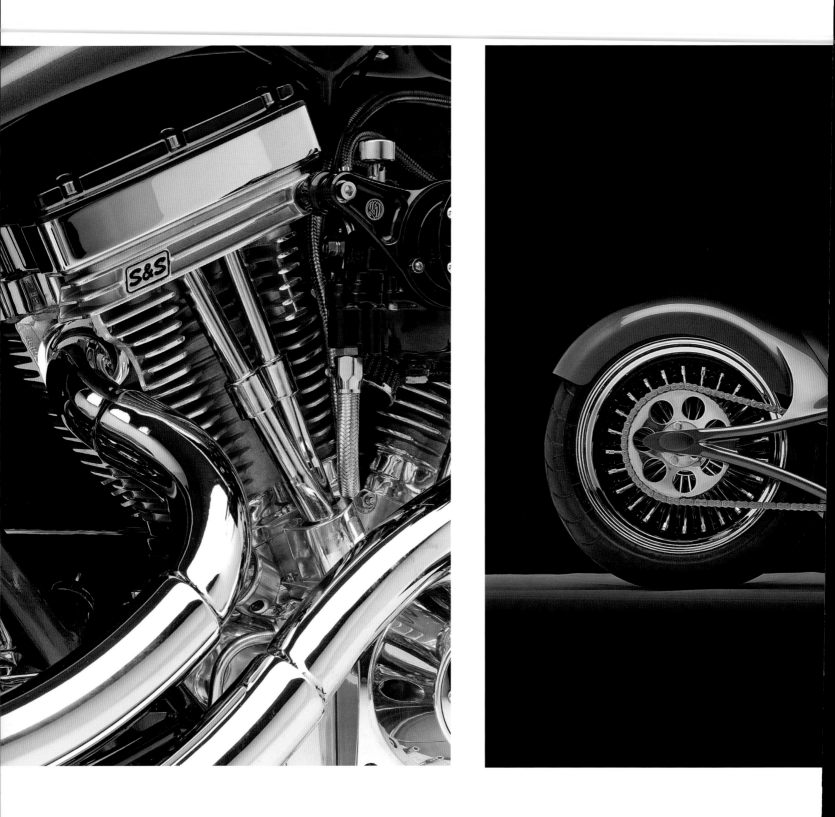

Section V

T-series Engines

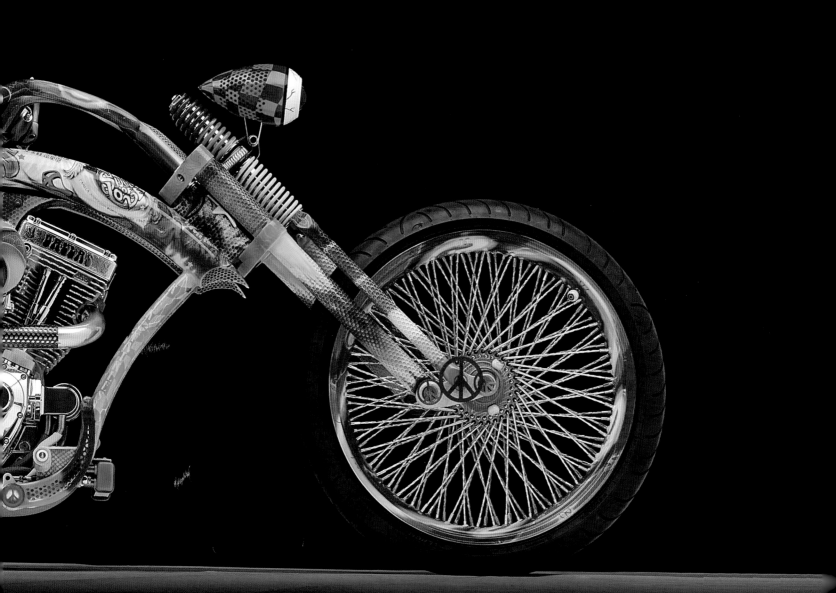

bennett's performance

G1

BENNETT'S PERFORMANCE DOESN'T OFTEN BUILD MOTORCYCLES. It focuses its energy and skills on engine work—installing performance parts or doing custom performance tuning—not building custom bikes. It also likes to go racing at the drag strip and at Bonneville, which is something it has in common with S&S.

Starting with a Kenny Boyce Pro Street frame that featured 35 degrees of rake and 2 inches of forward stretch, the Bennetts added an RMD Billet girder fork assembly. In the rear, a Chopper Guys swingarm and rear suspension from Works Performance completed the chassis. Dunlop high-speed rated tires were spooned onto Performance Machine wheels, an 18-inch front with a 17 out back.

Now the Bennetts needed to add the skin of a race bike to surround the D&D aluminum gas tank. They looked in the Airtech catalog, came up with a fairing and tail section that would work, and fit it to the bike. The Bennetts built the faux oil tank to house electronics and turned their attention to the engine.

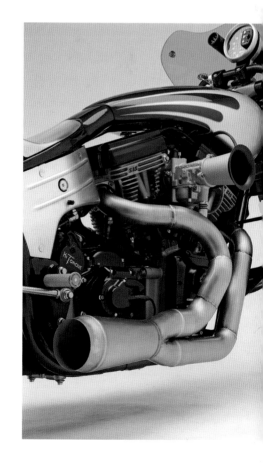

Bob ordered the S&S/G2 126-ci T-Series engine unassembled. When the box of parts arrived, they closed the door of the shop and went to work using secrets and tricks they had developed over the years that have never been and will never be, seen by anyone else. We do know that a Burns Stainless two-into-one exhaust and a Daytona twin Tec/MSD Ignition found homes on the engine. Transferring the vast amount of power from the engine to the back wheel is done with an Evolution primary, Rivera Pro Clutch with a lockup, and a Screamin' Eagle six-speed transmission.

Jon's Body Shop applied the paint, while Bob Iverson and Dan Harvill took care of the graphics and lettering. Gard Hollinger of L.A. Choprods built the seat to look good and hold Eric in place when he went to Bonneville with this bike.

Chapter 37

Rick Fairless

Pam

IMAGINE SITTING BEHIND A KEYBOARD LOOKING AT PICTURES OF THE NEW CREATION FROM THE MIND OF RICK FAIRLESS, *Pam*. What would you start talking about? The paint? The style? The details that pop up everywhere you look? Tough call, huh?

There is no mistaking Fairless' style; from his t-shirts to his Chuck Taylors to his paintwork, the man behind Strokers Dallas is easily recognizable. When asked to be in the S&S 50th Anniversary, Fairless was thrilled. He already had a new bike planned, and the event became the impetus for construction.

The Strokers team went to work on a frame that would feature built-in oil and gas tanks. The steering neck ended up at 45 degrees with what would be considered 3 inches of stretch in the backbone. The wild creation was mated to a Rolling Thunder springer built 2 inches under up front, and the Strokers swingarm was connected to the chassis with a big hunk of tubing, as this bike is a rigid, even though it has the look of a Softail.

An S&S T-Series 124-ci engine connects to a BDL primary and a Baker six-speed transmission; however, you can't find the BDL primary in any catalog. It, like so many other components on this bike, has received a screen treatment that adds style—and extra real estate for paintwork.

The paint on *Pam* is as wild as anyone has ever seen. Look at it from any angle and you will find a new detail you didn't notice the last time you looked at it. Inside the wheel rim, behind the rear frame section, on the engine, and even on the forward controls, you'll find a full dose of the wild artistic capabilities of Other Side Customs.

Still, there is so much more to *Pam* than paint: the overall profile, the screen in place of sheet metal, the 20- and 23-inch wheels, the exhaust that seems to disappear behind the engine. Clearly this is a bike that begs you to take your time, look over it closely, and then sit back and wonder how Fairless dreams up something like this.

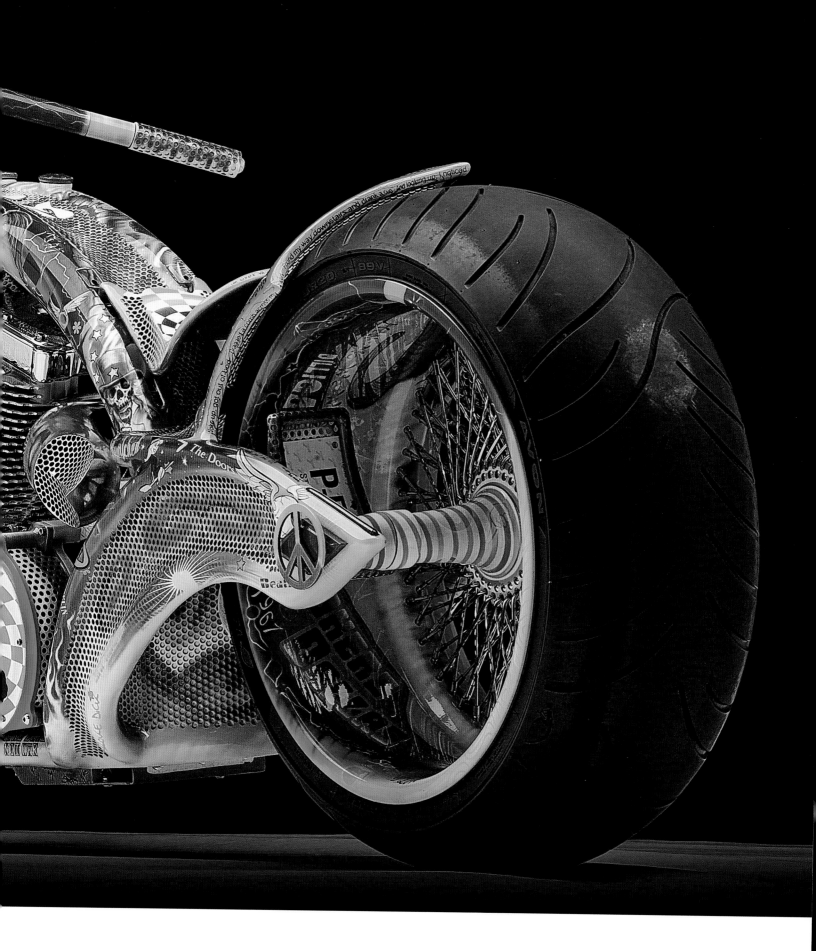

Chapter 38

G2 Motorsports
G2 Custom

Fast, faster, and fastest are the categories from which you can order a bike from G2 Motorsports. There is no regular, and certainly no stock, just various levels of ridiculously fast. It is not uncommon to see full-dress baggers with an S&S/G2 126-ci twin cam engine putting 150-plus horsepower to the rear wheel. Take that same engine and put it in a racy chassis like this bike, and you have a recipe for big fun.

The platform for the *G2 Custom* is a frame G2 Motorsports produces, with 28 degrees of rake, 2 inches of stretch, and a 6-inch extended swingarm. Wheels are super-lightweight Marchesini wrapped up in a Metzeler front tire and a Mickey Thompson rear. Suspension is also premium: a Paoli fork assembly and a pair of Progressive Suspension shocks.

Make no mistake about it, the S&S/G2 126-ci engine is a monster with a bore-and-stroke figure of 4.375x4.187 inches, but it is as docile on the street as you could ask for. A nice, lumpy idle gives way to the scream of horsepower from the Rush Racing/G2 exhaust as it revs right up to redline with no hesitation. The big-bore, short-stroke engine feeds power through a chain primary to an S&S helical gear six-speed transmission.

To keep weight down, there is not much to the bodywork on the bike. A carbon fiber front fender, G2 gangster gas tank, under-seat surround panels, and a G2 rear fender are all it takes to give this bike a sleek look. The addition of the chin spoiler enhances the racy look.

The significance of this bike goes even deeper than just being part of the S&S 50th Anniversary. It was also the subject of a two-part television show on *Horsepower TV*, where students at WyoTech built the bike to be part of the celebration, after which it traveled around the country for fans of the show to see.

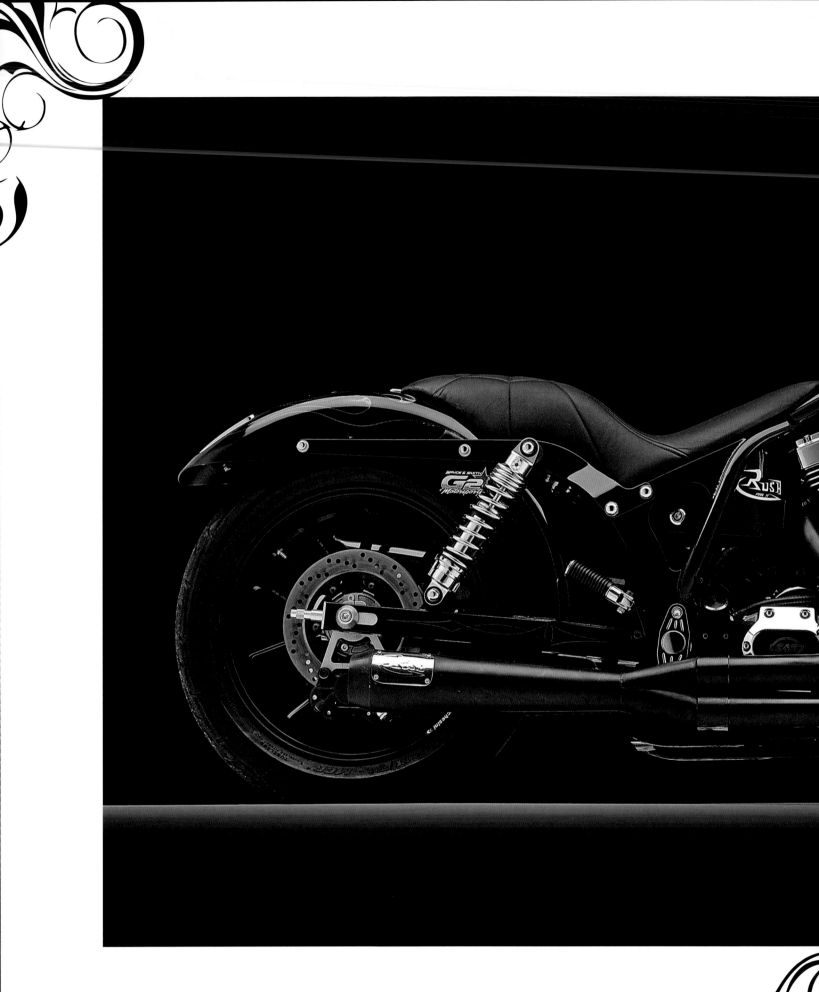

Chapter 39

Dan Roche
NC Machine

If you ever want a long period of time to build a bike, move next to Dan Roche in Manitoba, Canada. It's cold up there, which makes for a really long winter. While this cuts into riding time, it does allow a lot of time to get a project done. Roche has built more than his share of bikes featured in magazines, so he knows how to use the downtime to his advantage. His creation for the S&S 50th Anniversary clearly shows he had a productive winter.

Starting with a Daytec Raptor frame, Roche put his plan in motion. First, he mounted a 10-inch-over Rolling Thunder springer to the 40-degree neck, maximizing the length that the extra 6 inches of stretch in the frame produced. To get his new chopper rolling, Roche wrapped Performance Machine wheels—21- and 18-inchers—in Avon tires. While shopping at Performance Machine, Roche picked up four-piston calipers with the same design as the wheels to squeeze the rotors at both ends.

Next, Roche slid the S&S T124 engine into the frame. He equipped it with the all-new S&S Super G carb on an S&S Single Bore Tuned Induction intake. A set of Ness pipes was added to maximize performance.

A Primo belt drive primary with a lockup clutch connected to a Baker six-speed transmission with right-side output gets the power to the ground. There is no doubt Roche takes performance seriously; his transmission is equipped with an ignition kill so he can shift at full throttle—without the clutch!

To dress up his ride, Roche and Maurice Cahill ordered a pair of fenders from Russ Wernimont and a gas and oil tank from Daytec. These components were nice pieces as delivered, but Cahill and Roche did a little of this, and a little of that, to create exactly the right profile for the bike. Their hard work resulted in a beautiful platform for the Cahill Autobody cobalt-blue and Saab-blue paint job.

Once the paint was dry, Roche incorporated a Dakota Digital gauge into his handmade bars, Performance Machine hand and foot controls, Ness lighting, and a Corbin seat. The end result is a gorgeous bike that turned a potentially long, cold winter into a hot chopper.

walz Hardcore cycles
Ferrari Bike

WITH A DECIDEDLY PERFORMANCE-DRIVEN EDGE TO HIS DESIGNS, Marcus Walz has been making his name known around the world for years now. While it seemed everyone around him was out to build the flashiest, most attention-getting bikes around, Walz was building bikes that drew inspiration from performance automobiles.

His creation for the S&S 50th Anniversary event drew heavily from the most famous Italian auto manufacturer—Ferrari. On a racy bike like this, the only option for wheels had to be a set made in-house at Walz Hardcore Cycles (WHC). The aluminum beauties were anodized black, wrapped up with Metzeler rubber, and given beefy rotors for Brembo radial calipers to squeeze. An extra cool touch was the addition of a "knock-off" hub for the rear wheel.

Power for the sport machine comes from an S&S T124, pushing some 130-plus horsepower and almost 140 lb-ft of torque to the rear wheel through a Baker primary and six-speed transmission. The pipes and air cleaner are WHC pieces, fitting the design of the bike perfectly.

A tiny fairing surrounds the Yamaha headlight, and a WHC front fender and gas tank round out the paintable pieces. A flat red paint scheme covers everything but the front fender, which is black with red, white, and green stripes—a tribute to Italian carmakers.

Walz scored a high-speed home run with this bike. Like the Ferrari it is intended to resemble, it looks fast even when sitting still.

Section VI

x-series engines

Chapter 41
Big Bear Choppers

Scroll through the Big Bear Choppers (BBC) website and you will find a complete line of choppers and pro street bikes that scream custom. Long and low, with fat back tires and plenty of fancy paint and chrome, they look just like what you would expect production custom bikes to look like. Kevin Alsop, owner of BBC, knows what his customers want and gives it to them.

Alsop also likes to indulge his creative side and build bikes that teach him a little more about design. Together with his in-house design guy, Keith Garcia, Alsop created concept drawings for a sporty bike that incorporated a big V-twin engine. The look was a clear street racer with just a touch of industrial cool.

Everything was built at BBC, starting with an unusual frame that has only 30 degrees of rake. The frame stretches 3 inches in the middle to add length to the wheelbase without creating a chopper-esque look near the steering neck. An Ohlins fork in BBC trees rides up front, while a BBC swingarm that is stretched 6 inches connects to an Ohlins shock mounted vertically in the rear.

The proportions of this new bike were enhanced greatly with the installation of 23-inch front and 20-inch rear wheels and Avon tires. BBC created radial mounts for the Brembo calipers and then turned its attention to installing the S&S X-Wedge built to BBC specifications. It completed the driveline with a BBC enclosed primary and a Baker six-speed.

An aluminum gas tank tops the frame, as you would expect, but Alsop and Garcia designed it to work as an air deflector, forcing air to the intake and ensuring the rear cylinder gets cool air. Thin and discreet carbon fiber fenders cling to the tires, while a full panel section gives the seat a prominent place to reside and a home for the oil tank.

From its polished swingarm to the gold-trimmed suspension components, the BBC sportbike catches your attention. The more you look at this design exercise, the more you want one for your garage.

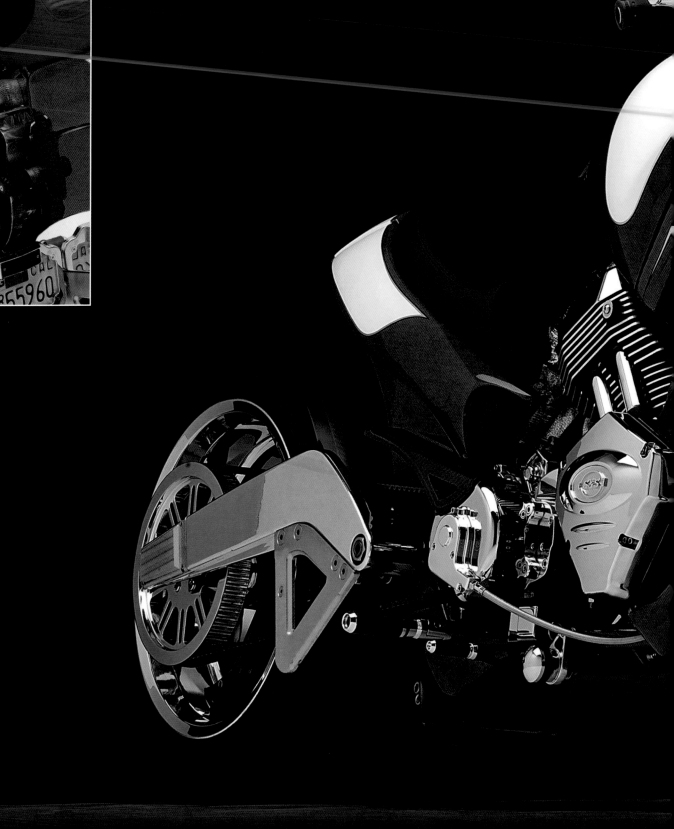

Chapter 42

Bourget's Bike Works
Magnum Fat Daddy

"STEALTH" IS THE WORD ROGER BOURGET USES TO DESCRIBE THIS BIKE, which is devoid of chrome, flashy paint, or any bright surfaces. While the lack of flash may make this bike stealthy, it's awfully hard not to notice a bike this long and powerful looking. Stealth, maybe—cool, definitely.

Bourget's Bike Works (BBW) has been building Fat Daddy models for years, but Magnum Fat Daddy marks the introduction of a model featuring the S&S X-Wedge engine. The chassis is big in size, big in tube diameter, and big in style. With 47 degrees of rake and 7 inches of stretch, the Fat Daddy bears the distinction of being one of the very first custom V-twins to carry oil in the frame.

BBW did the chassis properly. A BBW springer that is 10 inches over stock rides up front, and a pair of Progressive Suspension shocks holds up the rear. A set of Avon Venom tires protects the three-spoke BBW wheels, 21- and 17-inch, and matching rotors. With the chassis set, the 117-ci, three-cam, 56-degree X-Wedge was installed.

Since the frame of a Fat Daddy carries the oil and does the rear fender duty, the big metalworking operation is based around the gas tank. Like the rest of the bike, it is huge, fitting under the backbone of the frame and filling up the area between the neck and the seat. Last is the addition of a tiny chin spoiler and small filler panels for the open area under the seat. This massive bike is still very minimal.

All of the parts on the bike were either powder-coated black or treated for a brushed aluminum finish. From the 3-inch extended forward controls and the handlebars, to the axle and pivot covers, everything has the subdued finish. I guess, looking closely at the Magnum Fat Daddy, you could call it stealthy, but you would only be fooling yourself if you thought that's all it was.

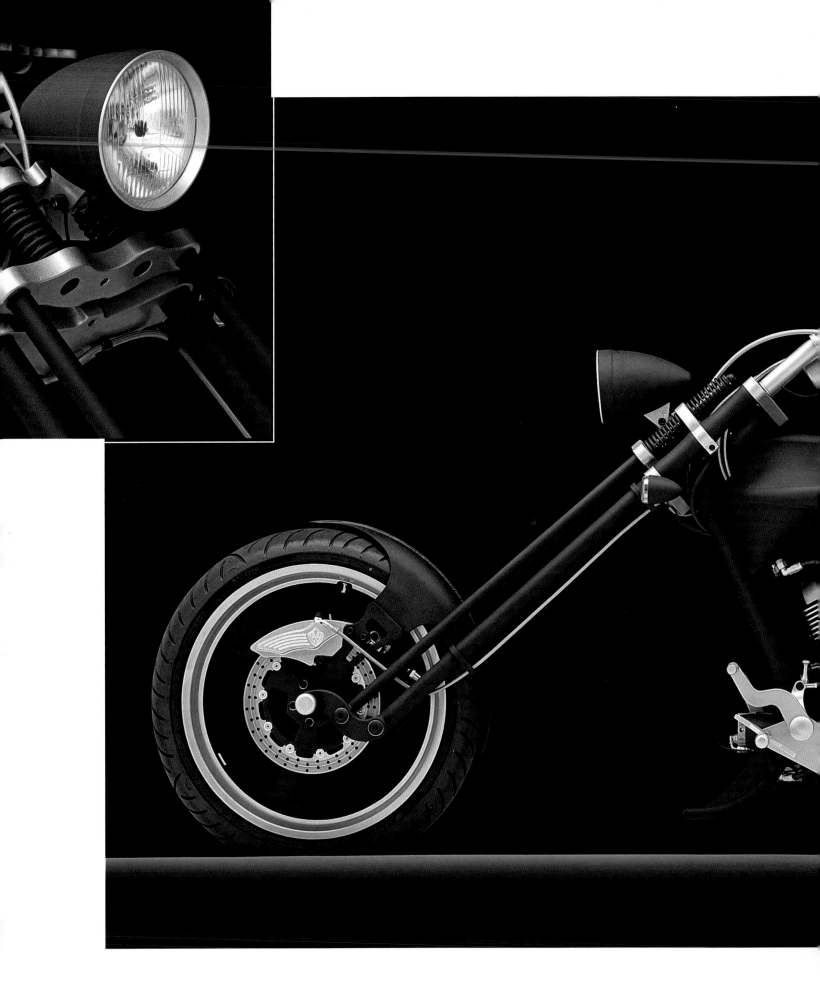

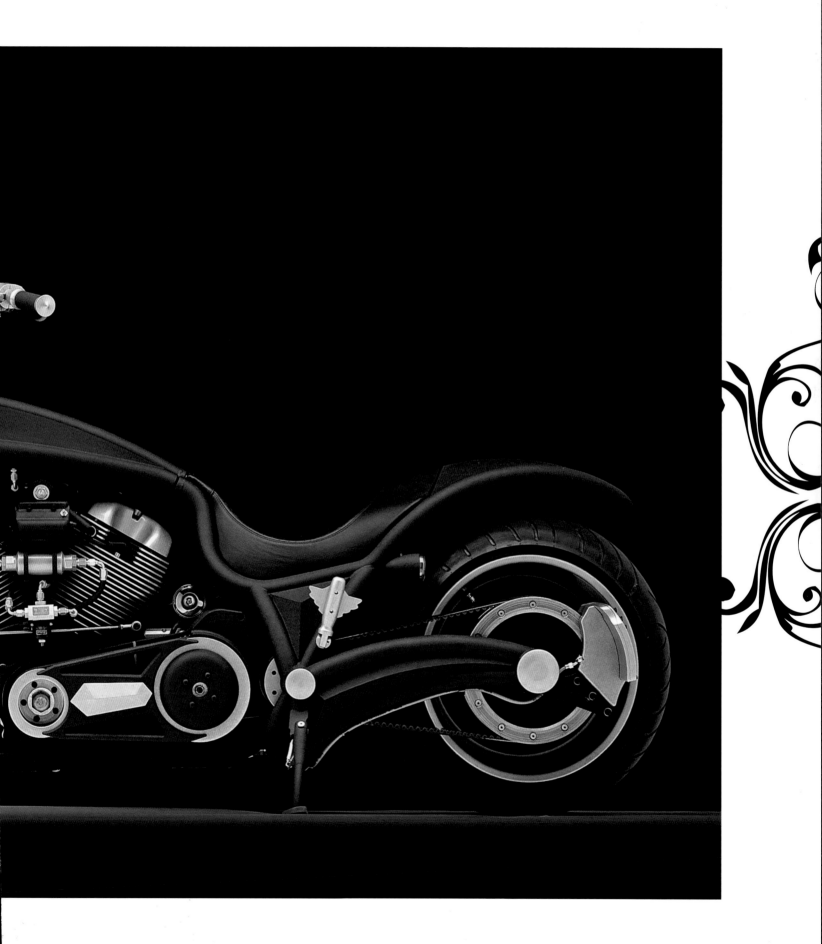

Chapter 43

Chopper Dave's Casting Company
Secret Weapon

CHOPPER DAVE HAS A COOL LITTLE SHOP IN HAWAIIAN GARDENS, CALIFORNIA. He focuses on vintage V-twins and street rods, not modern performance engines that are EPA compliant. Yet when S&S approached him about building a cool little bike based around its all-new X-Wedge—a 56-degree, three-cam proprietary design engine—he grabbed the opportunity.

Since the X-Wedge is not a typical V-twin, Dave started by working with BYC to create a frame that would accommodate the new engine mounts. Dave's philosophy is, "Why own it if you can't ride it?" so he had BYC set the neck at 30 degrees with no additional stretch in the frame.

Dave specializes in casting things, so when it was time to make the tanks for his bike, he looked no further than his own shop. The cast-aluminum tank sitting high atop the frame gives this bike its cool look, and the tagline "Powered by S&S" makes it even cooler. The oil tank bears an X-Wedge emblem, so everyone knows exactly what the central point of the bike is. A polished stainless steel rear fender and a Fab Kevin fork brace are all that separate Dave from road debris.

Now, about that X-Wedge: the 56-degree V-twin measures 117 ci and uses three belt-driven cams to regulate the engine's breathing. Fuel injectors supply fuel directly into the heads, and although you would never expect it on a bike like this, O_2 sensors ride in both pipes to complete the closed-loop fuel-injection system of the X-Wedge.

Chopper Dave jumped out of his comfort zone for this project, changing how people think about modern EPA-compliant engines and building a really cool bike along the way.

Chapter 44

Dougz custom paint and fabrication
Pro Tour X

"Yes, it's a bagger" will more than likely be your first thought when seeing this Dougz Custom Paint and Fabrication machine. But the *Pro Tour X*, born through the collaboration between bike owner Mark Platt and fabricator Doug Wozney, is much more than a "bagger."

Platt brought to Doug his idea of building an X-Wedge-powered custom that would be fun to ride, while Wozney had a plan for an over-the-top bagger. A few meetings and discussions later, the pair designed a bike. Wozney reached out to Rolling Thunder for a rubber-mount frame that would form the basis of the project. Geometry would be set to favor riding: a scant 30 degrees in the neck and no upward stretch, but 3 additional inches in the backbone to create a long stance and spread out the components.

Bodywork fabrication was where Doug outdid himself. He built the gas tank and front fender, modified the fairing to fit, and then took a moment to plan the tail section. His proprietary design incorporated a fender and saddle bags that are 8 inches narrower than a standard bagger, but offer more storage and open up as a one-piece unit.

Doug is best known for his painting skills, and he did not disappoint on Platt's bike. The two-tone Sikkens paint is separated by what seems to be a scrolling graphic. Look closer and you will realize it is a continuous 50 logo, designed as a tribute to the S&S 50th Anniversary Celebration.

Immediately after the S&S 50th Anniversary Celebration, the bike went to a few more shows before it was finally released to Platt for riding, which is exactly what Platt did with it right up until winter hit his hometown in Wisconsin. This bike definitely represents a plan that came together beautifully.

Chapter 45
Aldo Querio Gianetto
Strega

WANT TO GO DRAG RACING? If you were inspired to do that when you looked at the bike Aldo Querio Gianetto of AQG in Italy built, then Gianetto did his job well. See, Gianetto associates S&S with going fast while being on a motorcycle. The type of racing best exemplifying that connection is drag racing, thus his *Strega* creation was born.

A drag bike is sleek, with minimal everything and extra nothing. Gianetto looked at pictures of old drag bikes with small gas tanks, bikes with long, thin, tubular tanks, and bikes that seemed to have no gas tanks at all. That tankless look struck him as particularly eye-catching and fast-looking. He started working with Zodiac on a special frame with 36 degrees of rake, no stretch, and a very pronounced neck. To the rigid frame Gianetto added a fork assembly from an H-D Deuce that he had shaved before coating it wrinkle black.

The S&S 50th was Gianetto's first opportunity to work with an X-Wedge engine. Prior to the engine's trip to Italy, it made a quick stop at Dougz Custom Paint and Fabrication in La Crosse, Wisconsin, for several coats of Ferrari Red paint. Once Gianetto possessed it, he installed it in the frame and connected it to a Baker six—no, make that seven-speed—transmission with a Performance Machine/BDL primary assembly. Wheels came from Performance Machine, as did the brakes, and the rubber was from Avon—making the bike a complete running roller.

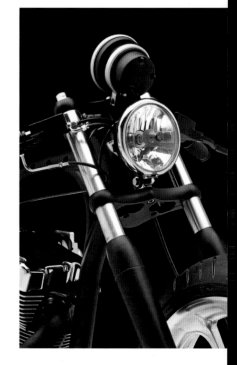

Aldo focused on sheet metal next—well, not too much focus, because he built a seat/rear fender/gas tank assembly to do it all. Then he built an oil tank that fit under the transmission, added the matte black paint, and turned his attention to the finishing pieces.

A set of AQG clip-on handlebars, a big dragster-style Auto Meter tach, Custom Tech hand controls, and Performance Machine mid-controls for the feet, Bates-style headlight, and an AQG taillight gave him all he needed to head out on the mean streets of Torino, Italy. A few miles around town and he knew he had built something that really paid tribute to S&S: a rideable drag bike.

Chapter 46
Kiwi Indian
Chieftain

TAKE TOO QUICK OF A LOOK AT THE *CHIEFTAIN* and you could easily dismiss it as a restored bike from days gone by. But to do so is to do yourself a disservice. This bike, an all-new 2008 model, was created by Mike Tomas of Kiwi Indian to show off just how old and new can come together for a mind-blowing machine.

Tomas, known in the motorcycle industry as "Kiwi Mike," is the keeper of the original Indian flame, making parts and doing restorations for those original bikes still on the road. He also builds new, ground-up bikes for customers, and in those, he has an opportunity to use today's technology to make them better—as with the *Chieftain*.

Using one of Kiwi Indian's plunger-style rear-suspension frames as a basis, Tomas built the engine and transmission mounts bigger and wider to accommodate an S&S X-Wedge. He set the neck at 27 degrees and connected a Kiwi girder fork with hydraulic damping to it. Knowing that he was going to ride this bike many, many miles, he built an additional device to add ride comfort: a hydraulically dampened seat post. Next, he slid 18-inch Performance Machine wheels with Avon tires onto both ends.

The S&S X-Wedge is a new engine, smooth, powerful, and designed to make plenty of torque at low rpm, so it was the perfect choice for this bike. Tomas connected the X-Wedge to the primary and five-speed transmission he worked with Sputhe Engineering to design. The assembly is shortened, compacted actually, to fit the frame properly.

There would be no mistaking the origin of this bike from its metal covering. Big fenders, calling back to the days when Indian bikes were everywhere, dominate the look of the bike. A combination gas tank/oil tank rides up top, with the oil tank taking advantage of the frame tubes to move the fluid to the engine.

The Kiwi red and cream paint added by Nostalgia Restyling completes the transformation from old to new. With just one motorcycle, Tomas and his *Chieftain* have crossed the boundaries of time, bringing the look of the 1940s to 2008.

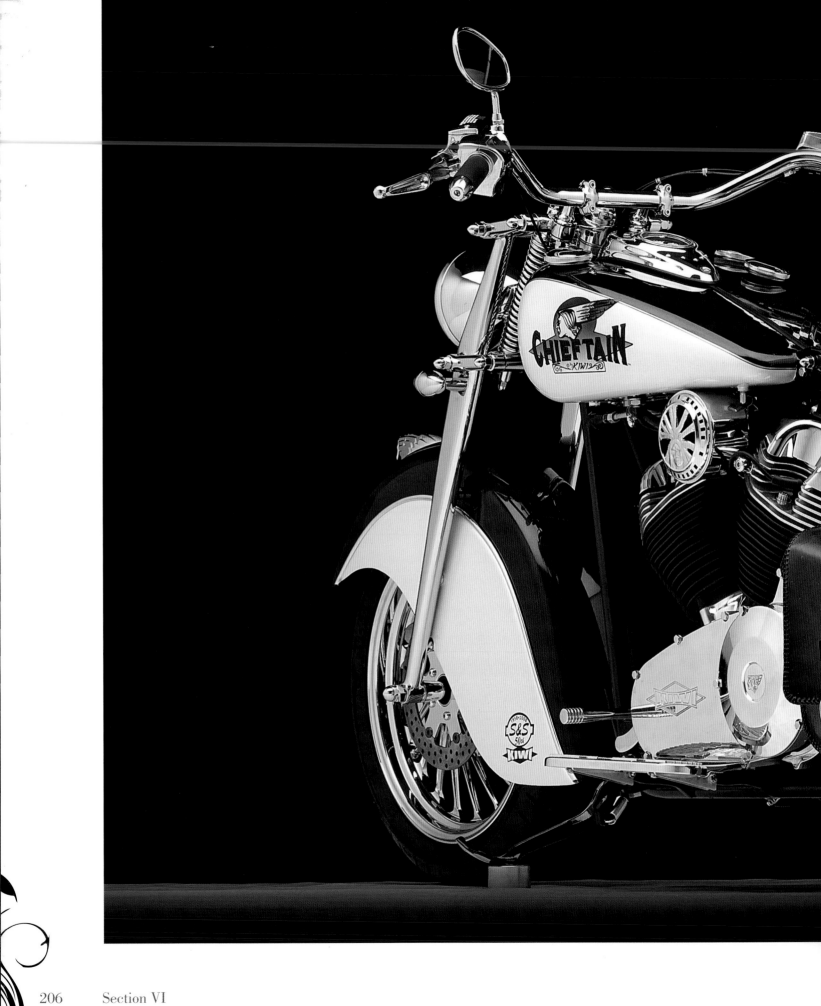

Chapter 47
klock werks
Swapmeet Louie

WHEN LOOKING OVER THE TECH SHEET ON BRIAN KLOCK'S BIKE, one line jumps out at you—"Build Time: 16 days." In Klock's defense, he was originally going to build a bike based on a Twin Cam engine, and then quite late in the program he did another builder a favor and swapped into an X-Wedge. The swap was both exciting and daunting, as it threw his whole original plan out the window.

Pacing the shop in deep thought, Klock and his crew piled up a host of parts and tried to picture the bike or come up with an idea for it. They went back and forth until Klock finally decided on using the original frame they had selected, a Rolling Thunder Twin Cam design with a 42-degree neck, 2 inches of stretch in the backbone, and the entirely wrong engine mounts. After they made the X-Wedge fit, it was on to more fabrication immediately, as time was running out.

First, the Klock Werks crew took a gas tank it had scored on eBay and built a new tunnel, dash, and filler panel for it. Then, since capacity was on the team members' minds, they built an oil tank that also served as a chin spoiler. Reaching onto their production inventory, a Klock Werks Thickster front fender was added to the front end, while another Klock Werks fender—the model didn't matter as it was cut to fit—was used in the rear.

The bike had a sleek look to it, but Klock wanted to add even more aggression to the stance. He rounded up a Buell XB fairing and adapted it to the front of the bike, transforming the mildly sporty machine into a bike that sends a clear message of speed. Back when he was first getting started in the custom world, Klock built a similarly styled bike, an FXR that everyone seemed to remember, so he dug out its paint code and had Customs Plus apply the Iris hue to his new machine.

Klock dropped a Danny Gray seat on the bike and did a test ride just 12 hours before the opening of the S&S 50th Anniversary show. Tired and worn out, Klock Werks built an amazing bike in the time it takes most people to plan one.

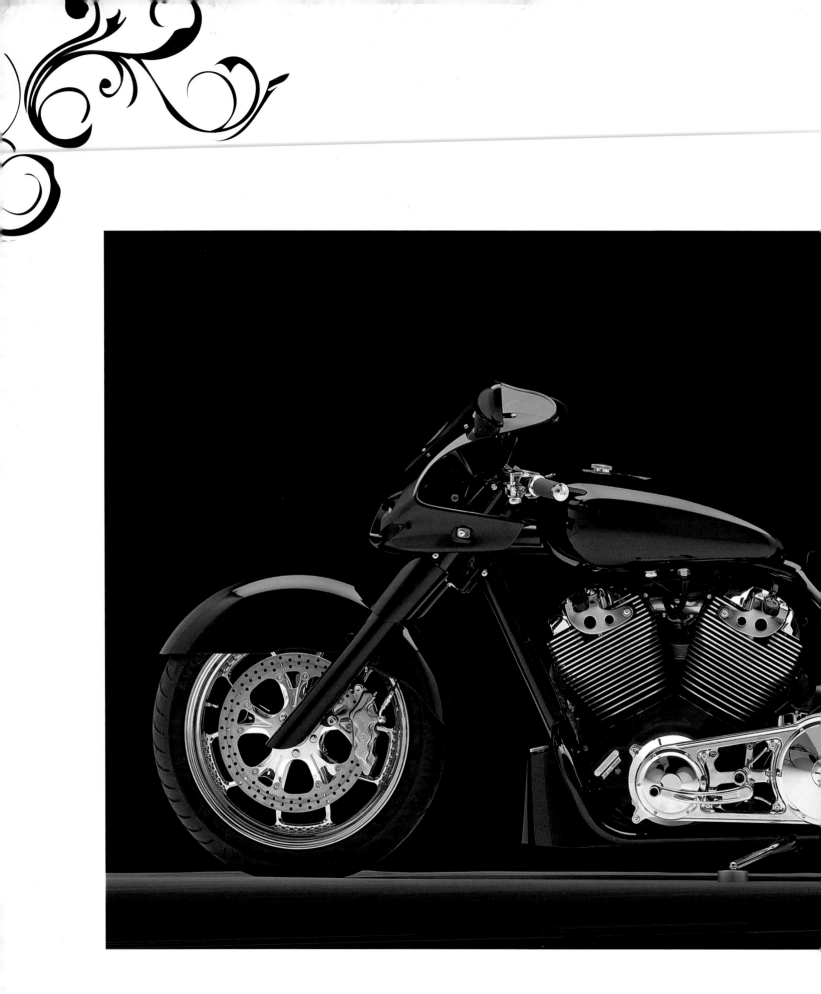

fred kodlin motorcycles
K-Wedge

DID YOU LOOK CLOSELY AT THE *K-WEDGE* BUILT BY FRED KODLIN MOTORCYCLES? Did you spend just a few seconds glancing at it, or did you really take some time to check it out? Hopefully you have a few minutes now to take in a bike that is clearly and certainly a one-of-a-kind.

When you are competing against 49 of the best custom builders in the world and you want to win, it takes unlimited creativity to build something different from the same old custom. Kodlin started things out differently by working with an idea to mount the engine facing 180 degrees opposite the norm. This would pose a few challenges in getting the drive to the rear wheel, as well as require extensive modifications to the frame configuration. Kodlin jumped on the frame design, incorporating a swingarm and fork design that was single sided, which added to the unique look of a "backwards" engine installation.

Since he was using the all-new S&S X-Wedge in his bike, doing something unique made sense. The engine is a 56-degree design, featuring three cams that are belt driven and fuel injectors that fire directly into the heads—not your everyday V-twin at all, and perfect for Kodlin's intent.

Kodlin worked with Primo and Baker to figure out the reverse direction of the primary and transmission. A look at the back wheel shows no rotor or caliper, no belt or chain; it appears to be free-rolling—however, it is not free-wheeling. Kodlin mounted a rotor and caliper to the transmission output and created a friction drive system for the rear wheel, therefore adding to the complexity of his bike.

Once the engineering was figured out, Kodlin built all of the sheet metal, controls, and, well, everything else you see on the bike. Take the time necessary to soak in the details and the overall impact. It is hard to describe the strength of Kodlin's design, but this is clearly a bike you can see yourself riding—or displaying in your house as you would be tempted to do with a one-of-a-kind work of art.

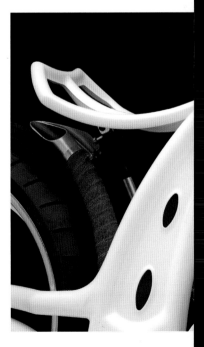

Chapter 49

orange county choppers

TELEVISION IS A WONDERFUL TOOL FOR GETTING YOUR MESSAGE OUT TO THE MASSES. *American Chopper*, the Orange County Choppers (OCC) television series, tells the world that the shop builds wild theme-based choppers. If you can conceive a theme for a chopper, some corporation or other has probably asked OCC to build a bike based around it. Paul Teutel Sr. and his son, Paul Jr., have traveled the world promoting custom-built theme bikes and their TV show. It has brought them great success and notoriety, although, sadly, it has typecast them as exclusively chopper guys.

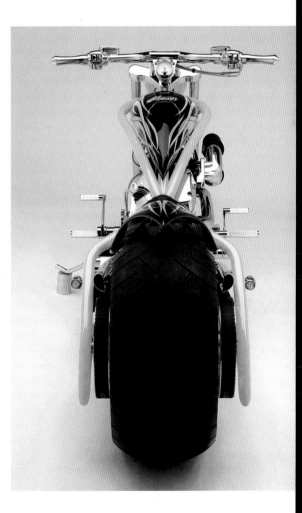

When they signed on for the S&S 50th Anniversary, the Teutels knew they would build something different than what anyone would expect. In order to ensure that the bike was different than anything else they had done, they used an S&S X-Wedge engine; the 56-degree package would force a new frame design, and from there they could go wild.

The Teutels fabricated an OCC gas tank to fit within the frame rails and sit very low over the engine, thus enhancing the massive look of the perimeter-style frame. To finish up the bodywork, a seat pan/rear fender/oil tank was built and fit with a Danny Gray seat.

Once the vivid yellow paint and flame graphics were applied and the chrome OCC controls and trim pieces put in place, the last operation came about, which was installing an exhaust system crossed in an "X" (a tribute to the modern engine) under the seat. There was no doubt in the minds of anyone at the OCC shop that this bike had broken out of the mold and into new ground.

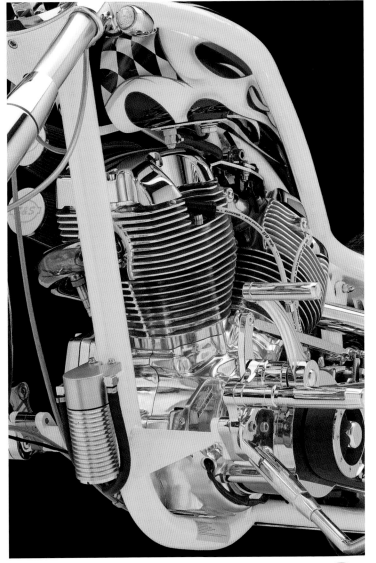

Chapter 50

Road Rage custom
S&S Anniversary Special

RAY PRATT, DAVE ANDERSON, AND THE TEAM AT ROAD RAGE CUSTOM IN NEW ZEALAND have a different view of what a custom bike should be. Custom means faster, better handling, more fun to ride, and generally made to bring a huge smile to your face. And it should push the limits of conventional engineering.

Starting with an S&S X-Wedge engine that was a 56-degree V-twin with three belt drive cams, oversize cooling fins, side-by-side rods, and a host of other technical upgrades from a 45-degree engine, the team planned a sportbike—fast, great handling, and completely different from anything else the team expected to see. Road Rage Custom built a frame that incorporated the engine as a stressed member and featured a 28-degree neck atop a single downtube. After carving out a set of triple trees from T6 alloy, the crew added 49mm fork legs. The swingarm is supported with a single Works Performance shock and the wheels—a 19-inch front and 18-inch rear, both fit with perimeter brakes—were made in the Road Rage facility.

Moving onto the bodywork, a combination rear fender/seat pan/gas tank was built and equipped with a customized 1958 Chevy taillight. The would-be gas tank is actually an air box and housing for all the electronics, adding a sense of normalcy to the bike's look. Examining the bike closely, those who know will recognize the custom-made primary cases, the stacked transmission, the custom case to house the six-speed gear set, and the exhaust canister designed to fit just under the engine case.

Pratt and Anderson worked closely on things like the handlebar and footpeg placement to get the ergonomics perfect on the bike. They wanted it sporty, but with enough comfort to really get out and spend time on it. While the bike looks small in photos, in person it is perfectly sized for its intended uses—being custom, going fast, looking good, and having fun.

221

www.amps.co.nz

SNS58

Auckland Motorcycles & Power Sports

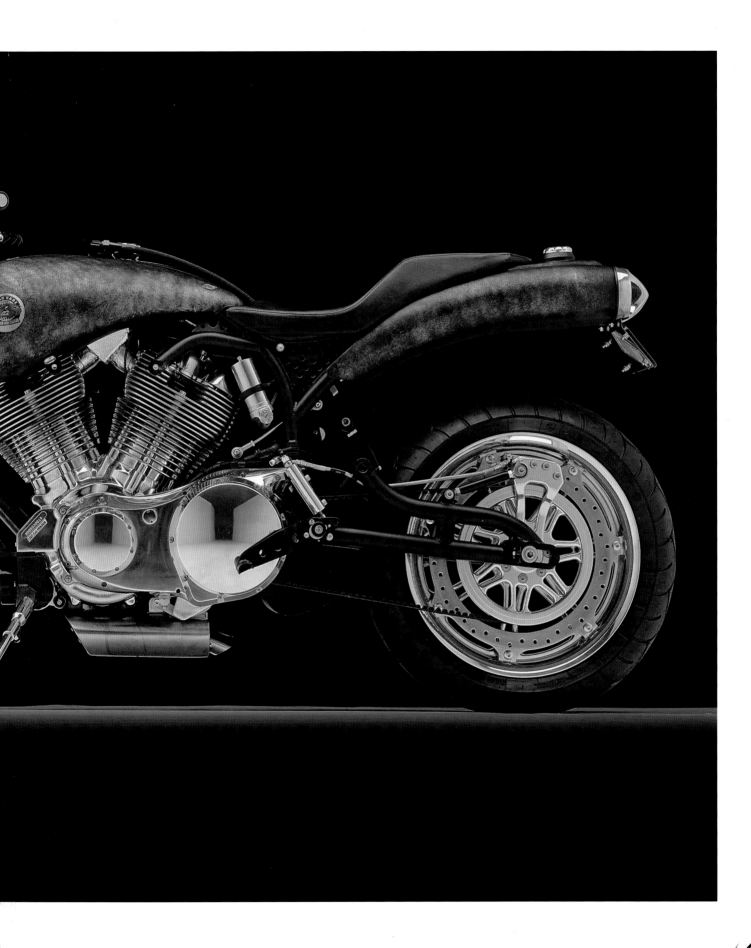